Planning for Long-Term Care

United Seniors Health Council (USHC), a program of the nonprofit organization The National Council on the Aging, Inc., is composed of thousands of consumers and professionals throughout the country who believe informed consumers are those best able to help themselves. In the 1980s, a few forward-looking people began to focus on the fact that changing demographics would create an increasing demand for nursing homes and other forms of long-term care. The catastrophic costs of long-term care (nursing home care, assisted living, home care, and community-based services) are well documented. The average annual cost of a nursing home is close to $55,000 and is expected to rise to $190,000 by 2030. Since Medicare covers little long-term care, that remains one of the largest out-of-pocket expenses for elders and their families. USHC was a pioneer in helping policymakers and consumers become aware of this vast problem. Since 1987, when USHC received a grant from the U.S. Administration on Aging to produce a consumer guide about long-term care, USHC has been actively involved in educating consumers and professionals about long-term care.

United Seniors Health Council
409 Third Street, SW
Washington, DC
www.unitedseniorshealth.org

Planning for Long-Term Care

United Seniors Health Council

A program of
The National Council on the Aging, Inc.,
Washington, DC

McGraw-Hill
New York   Chicago   San Francisco
Lisbon   London   Madrid   Mexico City
Milan   New Delhi   San Juan   Seoul
Singapore   Sydney   Toronto

Library of Congress Cataloging-in Publication Data

Planning for long-term care / United Seniors Health Council.—Rev. ed.
    p. cm.
    Rev. ed. of: Long-term care planning. Washington, D.C. : United Seniors Health Cooperative, 1997.
    Includes index.
    ISBN 0-07-139848-1 (alk. paper)
    1. Aged—Long-term care—United States—Costs. 2. Nursing home care—United States—Costs. 3. Aged—United States—Finance, Personal. I. United Seniors Health Council (U.S.)

RA644.6 .L668 2002
362.1'6'0973—dc21

                                   2002020219

McGraw-Hill

A Division of The McGraw·Hill Companies

2 3 4 5 6 7 8 9 0 DOC/DOC 0 9 8 7 6 5 4 3 2

ISBN 0-07-139848-1

This book was set in Trump Mediaeval by Patricia Wallenburg at TypeWriting.

Printed and bound by R. R. Donnelley & Sons Company.

This publication is designed to provide accurate and authoritative information in regard to the subject matter covered. It is sold with the understanding that neither the author nor the publisher is engaged in rendering legal, accounting, futures/securities trading, or other professional service. If legal advice or other expert assistance is required, the services of a competent professional person should be sought.

> *—From a Declaration of Principles jointly adopted by a Committee of the American Bar Association and a Committee of Publishers*

McGraw-Hill books are available at special quantity discounts to use as premiums and sales promotions, or for use in corporate training programs. For more information, please write to the Director of Special Sales, Professional Publishing, McGraw-Hill, Two Penn Plaza, New York, NY 10121-2298. Or contact your local bookstore.

This book is printed on recycled, acid-free paper containing a minimum of 50% recycled, de-inked fiber.

Dedication

The late consumer advocate Esther Peterson foresaw the coming need for accurate, comprehensive, readable information to help older people and their families make sound decisions about health insurance, home care, long-term care, and other health-related issues affecting older people. As cofounder of the United Seniors Health Cooperative (USHC), she spearheaded the organization's efforts to provide such information. This book on long-term care continues the values and high standards set by Mrs. Peterson.

Ensuring that persons have access to quality long-term care is becoming an increasingly important consumer issue for older people and their families. It also can be a complex issue, involving the use of family resources, the desire to remain living at home, the selection of the right level of supportive services and living arrangements, and decisions about buying long-term care insurance.

This book provides the information and guidance people will need to make sound decisions about ensuring and gaining access to long-term care. It covers long-term care in the home, in supportive living arrangements, and in nursing homes. It discusses options for and factors that should guide a consumer's decision on purchasing long-term care insurance. It describes government programs that pay for long-term care and where a person can go for unbiased information.

I am pleased to recommend this book to older consumers and their families.

Ann Landers
Chicago, Illinois

Contents

Foreword

Because so many of us are living longer, almost every family faces challenges about how to arrange and pay for long-term care. Millions of older Americans are worried that they won't be able protect themselves from the potentially catastrophic costs of nursing home or in-home services. Within a few years, eldercare will replace childcare as the number one family issue for the baby boom generation. We baby boomers are worried about our own futures as well. What can we do to ensure that we will be able to control our destinies as we grow older?

Today, consumers who need long-term care face a bewildering range of service options, including assisted living, home care, adult day services, and nursing homes. Cumbersome regulations and shortages of qualified workers contribute to concerns about quality and cost. Options to pay for care are even more complicated: Are there public programs that can help? What about reverse mortgages? Is long-term care insurance a good option? What about self-insuring?

Planning for Long-Term Care is designed to help consumers like you understand your risks, sort through your service and financing options, and make the best possible choices for you and your family.

The United Seniors Health Council (USHC) first developed earlier versions of this book, under the title *Long-Term Care: A Dollar and Sense Guide*, in 1988 with the assistance of a grant from the U.S. Administration on Aging and then in 1993 with the support of a grant from the John A. Hartford Foundation. Susan Polniaszek, MPH, former director of National

Services at USHC, authored the first two editions. This edition—*Planning for Long-Term Care*—has a slightly different title than the earlier editions in order to emphasize its usefulness as a planning tool and to distinguish it from the previous editions. This book is more than a revised edition with updated facts and corrections. In 1995, Edmund H. Worthy, Ph.D., former president of USHC, played a key role in revising the old text and providing supplemental material. While drawing heavily on Ms. Polniaszek's work, this new publication contains substantial changes throughout, from additional new sections to fresh advice for consumers. This 2002 edition was prepared under the direction of Charles Mondin, director, United Seniors Health Council, Washington, D.C.

United Seniors Health Council, now a program of The National Council on the Aging, has received much acclaim over the past 15 years for providing older people and their families understandable and unbiased information about critical health and financial issues. This book is part of USHC's ongoing mission to assist people in becoming better-informed consumers.

With all of its publications, USHC seeks input from a broad range of experts and is grateful to the following individuals for their advice, review, and comments on different parts of this revised edition.

Laura Addington, CFP, MSFS
Addington Financial Group
Greenville, TX

Rona Bartelstone, LCSW, BCD, CMC
Rona Bartelstone Associates, Inc.
Fort Lauderdale, FL

Howard Bedlin
The National Council on the Aging
Washington, DC

Robert Blancato
Matz, Blancato & Associates
Washington, DC

Winthrop Cashdollar
Health Insurance Association of America
Washington, DC

John M. Cornman
Consultants On Purpose, LLC
Arlington, VA

John Cutler, Esq.
Office of Long-Term Care
U.S. Office of Personnel Management
Washington, DC

Walter Feldesman, Esq.
Brown Raysman Millstein Felder & Steiner
New York, NY

Lisa Gables
The National Council on the Aging
Washington, DC

Robert Gilliat, Esq.
United Seniors Health Council
Washington, DC

Janette Hoisington
The National Council on the Aging
Washington, DC

Gail Gibson Hunt
National Alliance for Caregiving
Bethesda, MD

Nancy P. Morith, CLU
N. P. Morith, Inc.
Princeton, NJ

Wendy Pellow, Esq.
National Association of Insurance Commissioners
Washington, DC

Anne Werner Richardson
United Seniors Health Council
Washington, DC

Marlene Schneider
Benefits*CheckUp*
The National Council on the Aging
New York, NY

Joseph Scinto, Esq.
United Seniors Health Council
Washington, DC

Lisa B. Stewart, MS
Lisa Stewart Consulting
Spring Valley, CA

H. Cassedy Sumrall, Jr., Esq., PA
Delray Beach, FL

Christine Tschummi, MA, LNHA
Chevy Chase, MD

Alexis Walter
United Seniors Health Council
Washington, DC

Roba Whiteley
The National Council on the Aging
Washington, DC

A very special thanks to Stan Hinden, a trusted colleague and author of *How to Retire Happy*, for referring us to his editor, Mary Glenn, at McGraw-Hill. We appreciate the guidance and support of Mary Glenn and Jane Palmieri, editing manager, at McGraw-Hill.

Readers are advised that some information contained in this guide may vary from state to state. Please consult local authorities for state regulations. Congress or state governments may revise public benefits programs in the future. (We certainly hope so!)

In the meantime, all of us must do what we can to help our loved ones and to prepare for our own later years. We sincerely hope that *Planning for Long-Term Care* will help you and your family become informed consumers who can make decisions that will contribute to your health, independence, and financial security.

James P. Firman, Ed.D.
President & CEO
The National Council on the Aging
Washington, DC

Introduction

As the number of Americans over age 65 increases, so does the number of innovative and creative lifestyles for older people. No longer do we stereotype older people as frail and feeble. Today we are healthier, more active, and more independent for many more years than our grandparents were. We are more educated about our health and nutrition, and medical science is contributing to the comfort of our twilight years. Older Americans are no longer hidden and unproductive. They are making a big impact on the social, economic, and political life of our nation.

At the same time, it is inevitable that many of us will need some type of long-term care at some time in our life. This care may range from a service as simple as sharing meals with others at a senior center to an expensive service such as a lengthy stay at a nursing home. Long-term care refers to the physical, medical, social, and financial support often needed later in life. The prospect of long-term care can be frightening because of the dramatic changes that can occur when we face illness and advanced age: financial loss and dependence on others to take care of our basic needs. Problems arise when we find ourselves in need of this assistance and are unprepared and uninformed about our options.

This book presents various options regarding financial support for long-term care. Several publications are available that discuss services involved in long-term care, but very few publications discuss how older persons or their adult children can pay for these services. The material that is available is written by organizations that are selling their solutions. This book is a consumer guide to financing long-term care. It presents various options and discusses the pros and cons of each. The goal of this guide is to help you answer these questions: What are our long-term care needs? And how will we pay for them? Planning for our later years involves guess-work. But it's reasonable to assume we will require some sort of care at some point in our lifetime. We know it can cost a great deal of money, whether it is provided at home or in an institution.

Even if your philosophy about financial planning is to live without a thought for the future, it's smart to know your options in case you find yourself in need of long-term care. This guide presents you with options. In planning for long-term care, infinite variables affect the length of time and type of services required. For individuals, there are differences in financial resources, amount and accessibility of family support, and health status. All this points to the need to custom-tailor your plan for financing long-term care to your unique situation. There is no one-size-fits-all solution.

Sometimes, in frustration, you may feel like saying, "Just tell me what to do!" You should be wary of those who are only too happy to make the decisions for you. Often you will find that they have their own special interests at heart and not yours. As with other major decisions in your life, you are the best person to make the choices that will best meet your particular needs.

Long-Term Care—What, Who, When, How Much?

Major questions often raised about long-term care are answered briefly in this overview. Information regarding long-term care services and alterna-tive means of paying for them is discussed in greater detail in the chap-ters that follow.

What Is Long-Term Care?

Long-term care refers to all the services available that make it possible for you to function as effectively as possible. We often think of long-term care as meeting only our medical needs. In fact, the kind of long-term care that you seek should meet your social, financial, and housing needs as well.

Long-term care is often incorrectly associated with the care of a person who is not expected to recover from an illness. Many people automati-cally assume that long-term care means "nursing home" care. Although long-term care includes nursing home care, it more commonly involves many other services. A number of these services are provided by friends and family members or are delivered to your home through community resources. Long-term care encompasses many services at various levels that can be matched to meet the unique needs of each person. For example, some people can cook their own food but may need assistance in shopping. Others may need help with the cooking, and still others may need to be fed.

Who Needs Long-Term Care and for What Reasons?

According to this broad definition of long-term care, everyone probably needs some form of it at some time. The form, duration, or kind of long-term care are different for each person and change with time. People of all ages use support services when recovering from an illness or an accident. These services are usually only needed temporarily. This guide addresses the long-term care needs of older people who may need these services temporarily or may need progressively more services for long periods as they age.

Physical impairment can affect a person's ability to perform basic activities of daily living. These basic activities are bathing, continence, dressing, eating, transferring, and using the toilet. Difficulties in dressing and bathing are the most common limitations. The ability to use the toilet and to transfer from one location to another are less common limitations. However, these require more frequent assistance. The ability to feed oneself is the last activity with which a person may need assistance. Someone might also need long-term care services because of cognitive impairment, which is limited intellectual awareness of surroundings and events. Physical ability may be fine, but constant supervision may be necessary to protect the person or others from harm. Physical or cognitive impairments may be the result of a medical condition or just old age.

When Should You Start to Plan for Long-Term Care?

It is never too early to start planning, and never too late. The sooner you start, the better. While long-term care is primarily a concern of the older population, the possibility of a chronic illness or disabling accident is ever present. Saving regularly during your working years can help you accumulate the financial resources needed for retirement and long-term care needs.

The flexibility of your long-term care plan is more important than its completeness. It should include financial assets and resources available from friends or family. You should state, in a health care directive or other legal document, your personal wishes regarding your care if you become unable to make those decisions yourself. As your needs change, reevaluate your plan and make the appropriate adjustments.

Who Provides Long-Term Care?

A variety of organizations and individuals provide long-term care. Providers include friends and family members, community volunteers, and professionals. Friends and family members who provide regular assistance are called informal caregivers. Assistance to relieve the informal caregiver is called respite care. This assistance can be a few hours in the home; all day in community facilities called adult day service centers; or short, temporary overnight stays in a nursing home or assisted living facility.

Social and religious organizations are an excellent source of social and physical assistance. Services, usually delivered by volunteers, are often provided free or at a nominal charge. Services range from socializing to assisting in maintaining the home, such as doing repairs or light housecleaning. These organizations are also an excellent source of referral to more professional assistance.

Professional providers of long-term care vary greatly in both their setting and service. Often, several long-term care professionals, which may include an elder-law attorney and a geriatric care manager, work together as a team. Services may be provided in a hospital, a residential institution, your home, or a facility within your community. Level of care may range from a homemaker for personal assistance or custodial care to a registered nurse or therapist for skilled care. It is important for you to distinguish between these levels of care and settings. The costs of these levels of care are considerably different and may not be covered by Medicare or insurance.

What Are Your Chances of Needing Long-Term Care in Your Lifetime?

Our nation is growing older. At least 6.4 million people aged 65 or older need long-term care, with 1 in 2 people over the age of 85 requiring such care. It is estimated that nearly 6 percent of all persons aged 65 and over are living in a nursing home. After the age of 85, half of us will need help with the ordinary activities of daily living (ADLs). One of the biggest risks for older people is Alzheimer's disease, which eventually requires full-time care. Approximately 1 in 10 persons over age 65, and nearly half of those over age 85, will get Alzheimer's disease.

Although you cannot predict when you will need long-term care or if you will need it at all, you should not ignore the possibility of needing it at some time in your life. The best solution is to secure a plan for care for the future.

How Much Does Long-Term Care Cost?

The cost of long-term care depends on the level of care and amount of service needed. Some social and physical assistance is free or provided at a nominal charge from social and religious groups. At the other end of the spectrum is the very expensive nursing home or home care services that today can cost $125 to $175 or more per day.

Medical care is expensive in the United States and continues to increase in cost faster than most other goods or services. To stretch your resources, select the long-term care solution most appropriate for your needs. For instance, if you only need assistance to prepare meals, specific services in the home may be more appropriate and less costly than entering an institution.

Financial Planning and Investing

The ability to pay for long-term care is a major concern for many people once they begin to plan for their later years. It is never too soon nor too late to plan and manage your finances no matter what the amount of your income and assets. When it comes to long-term care, your financial well-being is just as critical as your health.

This guide suggests a variety of ways to pay for long-term care. First, though, a general review of the basics of good financial management is in order.

Whether you have a small or large portfolio of investments and assets, your most important consideration is to protect it. You should avoid risky ventures and investments that are not likely to be profitable for several years. There are many good solid investment options in traditional sources, such as high-quality stocks and bonds or mutual funds, where the risk is comparatively low and the return acceptable. Definitely avoid get-rich-quick schemes and deals.

For many years conventional wisdom dictated that as people aged, they should shift their investment strategy from growth and blue-chip stocks to income-producing investments such as bonds, Treasury bills, and perhaps some utility stocks mixed with certificates of deposit. This simple strategy is not so appropriate for today. People are living longer than ever before, and many are also retiring earlier than in the past. Therefore, they need to plan for retirement income over a 10-, 20-, 30-, or sometimes even a 40-year period. During this time span there will be inflationary cycles and economic ups and downs. This calls for a flexible, broad-based strategy.

Here are 10 brief guidelines for you to use in developing your personal financial plan.

1. *Financial planning must be personal.* Newspapers, magazine articles, television talk shows, and even this guide can only give you guidelines and general direction. Your own personal situation is influenced by many factors, including the health of you and your partner, your personal finances, your employer-sponsored benefits, and your tolerance of risk. These circumstances are unique to you and should be treated as such.

2. *Evaluate investments with a critical business eye.* Do not hold stocks or other investments just because your dear old uncle used to work for the company or because he told you 20 years ago that the company was a great investment. The only thing worse than becoming too involved with your investments is to be too casual about them. Never "play" the market. Investing is serious business.

3. *Maintain a portfolio appropriate to its size.* If you have a small portfolio, you should consider investments in mutual funds over individual stocks. Individual stocks can, and sometimes do, become worthless. No mutual fund has become totally worthless. A fund's value can and will go up and down *but not* out of sight. With assets less than $100,000 to invest, mutual funds will give you the diversity, as well as professional management, you need.

4. *Equity assets are most appropriate as long-term investments.* If you expect to need your funds within 5 years (the short term), equity funds may not be the best investment choice for you. Although the S&P

Composite has enjoyed a 10-year return (January 1, 1990 through December 31, 2000) of 13.57 percent, the 5-year average return for 2000 was a negative 10.14 percent. If your need is short term, you may not have the time to make up a loss of principal. Before making an investment, be certain the investment objective is consistent with your goals and time constraints.

5. *Investing and deferred spending (sometimes called savings) are different.* We all save for special things such as a vacation or a new car. Whatever the purpose, it is clear that we will spend that money at some point in the not-too-distant future. Putting $50 a pay period into your credit union toward a summer vacation is deferred spending. Putting that same money into your retirement fund is investing. The importance of this distinction is not to fool yourself that you are investing for the future when you really are deferring an expenditure.

6. *Income is only part of total return.* An investment can give you income, but the principal may be decreasing. This would cause you to end up with a worthless asset in the future. Beware of investments that include return of principal with your monthly distribution. A unit trust fund, for example, may have a high dividend payout because it is returning part of your principal. In these types of investments you actually run out of money at some future point. You cannot afford to be in this position during your later years when you may need resources for long-term care.

7. *Keep your eye on the bottom line.* In making investments, especially in mutual funds, many people get sidetracked with emotional issues like commissions, loads, and management fees. There is no free lunch in the investment world, so do not spend time looking for one. Your real concern with an investment should be its actual return. With lower commissions and fees you stand a better chance of getting a better return, but they do not guarantee a higher return. Look at the history of a mutual fund, the portfolio manager, or the broker who is making a claim and see what the actual money-in and money-out return was for several holding periods, including a bull market as well as a bear market. Also keep in mind that it isn't just what you make but what you keep that is important. You must consider the tax ramifications as well as the effects inflation may have on your portfolio.

8. *Do not confuse names with performance.* It may surprise you to know that the average total return on U.S. government bond funds for a 10-

year period from January 1990 through December 2000 was 8.87 percent. However, in 1999 this category lost 1.94 percent before bouncing back in 2000 with a return of 13.11 percent. It is important to note that even so-called safe investments may suffer loss of principal during times of market volatility. During this same 10-year period the average balanced fund turned in a 13.2 percent return, while the average growth fund returned 16.87 percent after sustaining a loss in 2000 of over 22 percent.

9. *Never invest in anything that makes you uncomfortable.* A mutual fund that has the words "U.S. Government" in its title may sound impressive, but this does not mean it will generate a good return. Intellectually we want to "buy low and sell high." However, if we react emotionally, we tend to do the opposite.

10. *Do not hesitate to seek help from an independent financial planner.* Your best choice is to turn to a certified financial planner (CFP) who will give you an opinion without selling you a product. It is acceptable to buy products from your adviser, but not until after objective advice is given. Be certain that the advice is specific enough that you can take it to someone else to buy the recommended investment, if you choose to do so. If the advice is complete and you have confidence in the adviser, there will be no need to go elsewhere. Through this process you can determine the degree of your adviser's interest in your welfare.

How to Use This Guide

The guide is divided into three parts. Part I discusses resources for living independently in your own home or in an assisted living environment. Part II discusses planning for the possibility of nursing home care. Both parts discuss long-term care services and present options of paying for the care. The last part, Part III, discusses a financial option available to help pay for long-term care in your home as well as in an assisted living facility and in a nursing home: long-term care insurance.

As this guide often stresses, long-term care does not just refer to nursing home care. In fact, Part I presents alternatives that allow you to remain in your home, alone or with assistance. This guide tells you what community resources are available and where to ask for assistance. It suggests some creative uses of your home and family to help you to live independently.

The possibility of needing nursing home care is a concern of us all. Part II prepares you for the decision about nursing home care and discusses how to pay for it.

Finally, carefully read Part III on long-term care insurance. This insurance product can help if you are healthy today and do not need long-term care in the immediate future. The cost will depend upon your age and other factors, and it may not be appropriate for everyone reading this guide. Part III helps you decide whether you need long-term care insurance and provides assistance in choosing an insurance policy that best meets your needs. If you are unsure about the benefit for yourself, seek independent advice.

For Your Information

The Financial Planning Association (FPA)
5775 Glenridge Drive, NE, Suite B-300
Atlanta, GA 30328
Phone: 800-282-PLAN
Web site: www.fpanet.org

The FPA is the membership organization for the financial planning community. It was created when the Institute of Certified Financial Planners (ICFP) and the International Association for Financial Planning (IAFP) unified in 2000. The FPA offers services and resources designed to help the public understand the importance of the financial planning process and can connect consumers with local certified financial planner (CFP) professionals.

National Association of Personal Financial Advisors (NAPFA)
355 West Dundee Road, Suite 200
Buffalo Grove, IL 60089
Phone: 888-FEE-ONLY
Web site: www.napafa.org

NAPFA is a professional association of comprehensive, fee-only financial planners. Members and affiliates provide consumers and institutions with comprehensive and objective financial advice on a fee-only basis. NAPFA provides consumers with information about financial planning and can refer consumers to planners in their area.

Society of Financial Service Professionals (SFSP)
270 South Bryn Mawr Avenue
Bryn Mawr, PA 19010
Phone: 888-243-2258
Web site: www.financialpro.org

The SFSP is a national organization of more than 30,000 insurance and financial services professionals who have completed educational courses and SFSP's programs.

Part I

Planning for Home Care

Keeping our independence is an important key to self-esteem as we age. We want to be free to choose our own lifestyle, whether that is continuing to live at home, moving to a retirement community, or sharing a home with family members.

Many of us fear that as we age, we will lose this independence because of medical or financial difficulties. We fear being placed in a nursing home or being forced to live away from our family and friends.

The need for long-term care does not mean that a person must be placed in an institution of some sort. Most long-term care assistance is provided in an older person's home or at a community facility such as a senior center or adult day service center.

The older we become, the more likely it is that we will need assistance with one or more regular, everyday activities of daily living such as eating, bathing, dressing, and getting out of a bed or chair. Some people may also need help with other activities such as managing money, transportation, or housecleaning.

Most of this personal assistance is provided by family and friends, who are sometimes called *informal* caregivers as opposed to *formal* caregivers such as home health nurses or adult day service center staff. Approximately two-thirds of all people receiving long-term care services at home or in the community are assisted by family members and friends. Almost one-fifth receive help from a mix of informal and formal caregivers, and 14 percent get help solely from formal caregivers.

The four chapters in Part I of this guide discuss different lifestyles and ways of financing them that will allow you to remain living in the community and receive long-term care services appropriate to your needs. Living arrangements range from staying in your home to moving into some type of shared living arrangement like a congregate housing facility that provides supportive services. Ways of financing long-term care at home and in the community include public and private insurance as well as comparatively new options like reverse equity mortgages.

I

Resources to Help You Live at Home

Most older people, if given the choice, would continue to live in their own homes as long as possible. Your home is convenient, familiar, comfortable, and close to friends and neighbors. Today, it is not necessary to move to a nursing home if you cannot manage all aspects of independent living. There are many other options.

Living independently means living in your own home or apartment or with family. Friends or family members are available to assist you when you need help, but otherwise you manage quite well on your own. Even in this situation, you may use long-term care services available in the community. You can take advantage of these services either occasionally or on a continuing basis. The important thing is to know what is available and how to request the services when the time comes that you need them.

The large majority of older people needing long-term care assistance of one kind or another continue to live in their homes and receive help from family and friends, who are sometimes called informal caregivers. When needed to augment the help provided by informal caregivers, a variety of community resources are also available. A key component of these community resources are home health care services. This chapter focuses on the combination of family and community resources for caregiving. Home health care services and ways to pay for them are discussed in Chapter 3.

Family As a Resource

The family unit is ideally designed to provide care and support for those who need assistance. About 70 percent of older, functionally limited Americans living in the community receive all their care from a spouse, child, or other relative; and 36 percent of these live with their children. The three top providers of care for those with limitations of daily activities are spouse (35.6 percent), daughter (32.6 percent), and son (17.1 percent).

Social changes in recent years, however, have affected the family's ability to care for family members who need help. Three changes creating the greatest impact are:

1. More women are working outside the home.
2. Family members often live in other communities or states.
3. The extended life span leaves a greater proportion of older people requiring support from the younger generation.

Aside from social changes, the three- and sometimes four-generational family household is strained by inflation, high medical costs, and limited housing. The "sandwich generation" feels a heavy burden in caring for both children and parents. Prospects, however, are not all gloomy. Often, all parts of the family benefit by pooling limited resources: financial, physical, and emotional. The essential factors for success are good communication and a profound respect for each other's needs and contributions.

Care can be arranged either in your home or in the caregiver's home. Ideally, the arrangement will allow you to retain as much independence as possible while limiting the physical burden placed on the caregiver.

Wherever the care is provided, every effort should be made to adjust the environment for ease and safety. Handrails, improved lighting, secured rugs, amplified telephones, bath rails, and other assistance help promote independence and save time for the caregiver. Many organizations such as the American Federation for the Blind, the Consumer Product Safety Commission, and local fire departments can suggest modifications to a home that enhance the safety and well-being of persons requiring assistance.

When long-term care plans include living with your children, you can augment their assistance with community services. An adult day service center enables the caregiver greater flexibility with a career and individual schedules. Visiting respite care and transportation assistance for medical appointments help you take greater responsibility for your own care. All these services help lift the burden of work and give both you and your caregiver leisure to enjoy life and each other.

Living with family is not a workable solution for everyone. Before a crisis occurs, discuss the situation with other family members. Sometimes children feel a parent is forced upon them. Other times, when children insist that a parent live with them, the parent knows the problems that can arise with too many adults in a household. A frank and honest discussion well ahead of time can avoid hurt feelings and misunderstandings.

Another possible alternative is to rely on your family for the financial support needed to pay for long-term care at home or in a nursing home. For some people this is a viable option, provided your family can afford the expense and you are willing to accept their help. However, it is important to discuss any possible decisions thoroughly.

You may take this arrangement one step further by giving your assets to your children in return for an explicit or implicit understanding that they will care for you for the rest of your life. When an individual gives someone a gift of more than $10,000 in any one year, there can be potential tax consequences, and so you should consult a financial adviser before giving away any large assets.

In order to meet Medicaid eligibility criteria for nursing home coverage without using up all resources, some people with more than average assets have considered giving most of them away to a relative or friend or transferring them into an irrevocable trust fund. In years past this could be accomplished more readily and with fewer consequences than today. According to current federal law, the fair market value of assets transferred to another individual within 36 months of your application for Medicaid is used to assess a period of ineligibility for Medicaid. The number of months of ineligibility is determined by dividing the value of the transferred assets by a state-determined average monthly cost of nursing home care. Recent federal law imposes penalties for inappropriate transfer of assets to become eligible for Medicaid. Because of the complications and possible liabilities of transferring assets, you and your family should consult an attorney familiar with elder-law issues before doing so. Chapter 6 of this guide provides additional information about Medicaid payments for long-term care and eligibility requirements.

The major drawback to giving your assets away is the loss of independence. You no longer have control over how your money is spent. Children may not provide the attention you thought they would give. Another major negative to giving your assets away is that they are subject to the legal and financial problems of the beneficiary, such as a divorce or lawsuit. Even when the assets are in a trust, they are considered community property in a divorce case or other legal matters.

Community Services As a Resource

A range of long-term care services are available in your community to enable you to remain in your home. Providing you do not need 24-hour supervision, you save money by remaining in your home and receiving only the services you need.

Each community offers long-term care services that differ in variety, price, and source. In order to learn more about services and providers in your community, call your local area agency on aging. You will find the number in the local government section of your telephone book under Aging Services, Department of Elder Affairs, or other similar names.

Area Agency on Aging

Your local area agency on aging receives federal funds under the Older Americans Act, which seeks to remove barriers to economic and personal independence for older persons and to assure the availability of appropriate community services for those persons in the greatest social or economic need. Each area agency on aging has flexibility in offering services to meet the needs of older people in its service area. Services fall into three major categories: home, community, and access.

- Services in the home include homemaker, chore service, and meal delivery. Through your area agency on aging or an organization providing the service for the agency, you may request services in your home. Professional staff discusses with you your particular needs and the services available to assist you. There may be economic eligibility requirements. In some communities there are waiting lists for publicly supported programs and services.

■ Services provided in the community include senior centers, adult day health care programs, nutritious meals served at community locations, protective services, and legal counseling. Legal assistance may include protection from financial or physical abuse, crime prevention, and victim assistance. Some communities offer legal representation on matters affecting Social Security, Medicare, and welfare benefits.

■ Access services include transportation to help older people travel to senior centers, medical services, Social Security offices, and shopping areas. Another essential service is information about and referral to appropriate community resources.

Since each community decides its own priorities among the needs of its residents, services vary from community to community. The Older Americans Act specifies that "an adequate proportion" of a local area agency on aging's funds be spent on access services, at-home services, and legal assistance. Therefore, services in your community may be very different from those offered in another community.

Although these services are quite valuable and are provided free or at very low rates, consumers should realize that they are not entitled to receive these services, unlike Medicare. The area agency on aging is expected to arrange for the provision of these services to the extent it is able. Therefore, you may not have access to services because the funds are not available.

Other Community Resources

Other sources of information about community resources include your physician, a discharge planner from a community hospital, local recreation centers, and community service groups. Your local area agency on aging may also suggest other appropriate community assistance.

Volunteer organizations within your community often have programs that serve older residents at little or no cost. Many religious organizations offer services or referrals to community resources. Check your telephone book for such organizations within your community.

Services offered may include homemaker service to assist in light housecleaning or personal assistance, chore service to assist with heavier chores in the house, and meals-on-wheels to deliver hot meals to the home for people unable to cook for themselves. Community pharmacies and grocery stores may provide home delivery, often free, within their service area. Volunteers often serve as companions or as the eyes and ears to events outside the home.

For people who are not homebound, but need assistance to reach needed services and providers, many communities offer senior discounts for transportation services. Some social service groups offer a volunteer to accompany an older person to medical appointments. Some communities have special transportation services for people who need wheelchair or handicap assistance.

Care Management Services

If you and your family find it difficult to locate, coordinate, or agree upon the best plan of care, you can seek out the services of a care manager or a care management organization. You can locate care managers through local area agencies on aging, through the National Association of Professional Geriatric Care Managers, or on the Internet.

The assistance of a care manager can be useful in a number of situations. For example, care managers can be most helpful when there are differences among family members about the most suitable course of action for an older parent or relative or when the family caregivers live at a distance or have too many competing demands to be able to manage the care. There are many other situations in which a care manager can be helpful, but the most important is when the family has concerns about care and needs guidance to assure they are doing the best they can.

The care manager can mobilize a single service or an entire team of providers to meet the individualized care needs of your situation. The process usually begins with a comprehensive assessment of the health, social, emotional, and physical needs of the older person. Then, working with the individual and family members, the care manager develops a care plan incorporating a package of services that most closely meets the needs, preferences, and resources of the individual and family. Most frequently these services are provided in the home, although it may even include selection of assisted living or long-term care facilities when that is needed.

At the option of you and your family, the care manager can implement and monitor the services to ensure quality, effectiveness, and efficiency.

The care manager can also continue to reassess the care needs so that the services can be increased or decreased when appropriate. An important component of the care manager's role is to provide education, advocacy, and emotional support to the person receiving care and the family. This helps to balance the needs of each family member.

The cost of care management varies. An initial assessment by a care manager can cost between $250 and $600. Ongoing supervision of care usually costs $70 to $200 per hour. Some public or nonprofit social service agencies may have sliding fee schedules based upon income.

When looking to hire a care manager, it is a good idea to ask the following questions:

What is the care manager's professional training that prepares her or him to work with elders?

What professional licenses or certifications does the care manager have?

How long has this person been in practice?

Is there an on-call system during evenings, weekends, and holidays for emergencies?

How does the care manager keep the family informed?

Which services does the care manager provide directly and which are arranged through an outside provider?

What do I do if I have questions or concerns about care?

Is there a written fee policy?

Are there references I can call who know your services and reputation?

Adult Day Services

An important and fast-growing part of the network of community resources that you and your family can access for help is the adult day services center. Most communities have these centers. They provide meals, health services, and recreational activities. Many programs also offer transportation.

There is a range of adult day programs, depending upon the level of care appropriate. The more medically based programs offer physical, occupational, and speech therapy and services from other health professionals. These adult day health centers provide frail older persons with a therapeutic and rehabilitative program, while at the same time offering relief for the caregiver. Some programs also have overnight respite services on a limited basis.

Less medically oriented programs usually do not offer therapeutic or health care services. Supervision is provided, meals are served, and recreational activities such as exercise, arts and crafts, and card games are available. Supervised staff provide daily assistance services.

The less medically oriented adult day programs may cost $25 to $40 per day and are not reimbursed by Medicare. Some programs charge a sliding fee scale based on ability to pay. The more medically based programs may cost $40 to $90 per day and may offer therapeutic services that can be partially reimbursable under Medicare Part B insurance.

Respite Care

The physical and emotional drain on the caregiver, who is often the spouse, is enormous. Respite care provides relief to the caregiver and can include a service such as someone coming to the home while the caregiver takes a nap or goes out for a while.

Respite care can also include adult day services as well as temporary overnight care in a nursing home or other institution. This allows the caregiver a vacation from the stress of caring for another person. Respite care in an institution may be as short as one night or as long as a week or two.

Funding may be obtained through Medicaid home and community-based waiver programs, the Department of Veteran Affairs, as well as some long-term care insurance policies.

For Your Information

Eldercare Locator
Phone: 800-677-1116
Web site: www.n4a.org

A free service provided by the National Association of Area Agencies on Aging and the National Association of State Units on Aging. Information specialists give callers the names and phone numbers of the most appropriate local information and referral resources.

National Adult Day Services Association (NADSA)
c/o The National Council on the Aging, Inc. (NCOA)
409 Third Street, SW, Suite 200
Washington, DC 20024
Phone: 202-479-6682
Web site: www.ncoa.org/nadsa

NADSA, an affiliated unit of NCOA, is an organization of professionals and agencies involved in adult day services. Like NCOA, NADSA serves as a resource for information. NCOA seeks to promote the well-being and contributions of older persons and to enhance the field of aging. A number of publications are available on topics of interest to adult day service providers. Write or call to obtain a catalog of publications.

National Association of Professional Geriatric Care Managers (NAPGCM)
1604 North Country Club Road
Tucson, AZ 85716
Phone: 520-881-8008
Web site: www.caremanager.org

NAPGCM has established a nationwide network of geriatric care managers to assist families who live far away from their older loved ones. Free referrals are available by sending a stamped, self-addressed legal-size envelope.

2

Your House As a Resource

When people reach the point of needing help with everyday activities, they often first consider entering a nursing home. This solution may be an overreaction to the problem and may well be unnecessary. Nursing home care disrupts your lifestyle and comfort and can be very expensive.

Fortunately, there are many alternatives for the 18 million older Americans who own their homes. The years and funds invested in your home may be used to provide you with a number of options to help you pay for long-term care needs.

Selling Your House

The simplest and most obvious use for your home is as a source of money. If you have cared for it well and you are located in a growing community, your house has likely appreciated in value. If, after careful evaluation, you find your greatest need is for cash and other considerations are secondary, you can always sell your house.

If you do not consider yourself a financial expert, protect your investment by consulting several qualified real estate agents to determine the fair market value of your home. Often people who have not recently bought property are so amazed by an offer much greater than their purchase price that they agree to sell their home for less than market value. Remember, since you have to purchase your health care and long-term care services at today's inflated prices, you want to realize the maximum price for your home.

> ## Uses of Money from the Sale of Your Home
>
> - Buy a home or condominium that is smaller, more convenient, or easier to maintain than your present home.
> - Move to an amiable climate.
> - Invest in a life care or continuing care retirement community (CCRC).
> - Pay for long-term care assistance in a shared living facility or nursing home.
> - Invest profits to produce continuous income.

The price you are paid for your house is *not* your net gain. You need to pay repair costs prior to selling, realtor's fees, and closing costs. The Taxpayers Relief Act permits home owners to exclude up to $250,000 of profit made on the sale of their principal residence from the capital gains tax ($500,000 for married taxpayers filing joint returns). This exclusion is not limited to any one sale, but can be taken every 2 years. This provision repealed the "once in a lifetime" exemption, whereby home owners over the age of 55 were allowed an exclusion of up to $125,000 of the overall profit made on the sale of their residence from the capital gains tax.

If you have paid off the mortgage and do not need the lump-sum distribution from selling the house, you may want to consider carrying the mortgage for the buyers. This will provide you with a steady stream of income that usually reflects a substantially higher rate of return than that obtained from a certificate of deposit (CD). Carrying a mortgage involves legal and financial considerations. You should be sure the buyers are financially qualified, and you ought to have an attorney prepare the contract and deed of trust.

Renting Your Home

As an alternative to selling your home, you might decide to rent it. This could be an excellent solution to paying for long-term care costs, provided that you need only regular income rather than the entire lump sum and that you have little or no mortgage on your existing home. You may want to use your home at a later time or leave it as an inheritance. Whether renting will generate sufficient funds for you can only be determined by someone with knowledge of your individual needs and property. You need to be certain that your rental income will pay any mortgages, taxes, and other expenses and still provide enough surplus income to cover your costs of long-term care.

A major disadvantage of renting is that you retain the responsibilities of being a landlord. You may avoid the physical, financial, and emotional effort associated with this role by renting to family members or a friend who would agree to maintain the property for you. The cost of repairs and general upkeep should be estimated and subtracted to determine your net monthly income. If you are absent or are unable or unwilling to perform the chores and duties of a landlord, you can hire a person or organization to act on your behalf. This will reduce your income, but the extra cost may be worth the freedom from responsibility.

Money received from rental property is income and is treated as such for tax purposes. However, you are allowed to subtract depreciation of the property and other expenses from the rental income received.

Taking in a Roomer

Another option is to rent only part of your home while you continue to live in it. This might be just a room, a whole floor, or a section of rooms that can be set aside as an apartment. As with housing arrangements, this can be as diverse as the individuals involved. Tailor your own arrangement based on your needs, preferences, finances, and housing situation.

Residential communities occasionally have zoning ordinances or restrictive covenants that may limit your plans for multiple occupancy. For instance, you may be allowed to rent a room or share your home, but not be allowed to establish a separate apartment. There may be fire and safety codes that dictate rules for a separate apartment. Find out the restrictions and regulations in your particular community before committing yourself.

Sharing with Family or a Friend

A common arrangement is to live with children or younger family members. However, when you are the house owner, it is reasonable to reverse the situation. Most families have someone who could benefit from such an arrangement: a student, a newly married couple, a working mother or a single person. The composition of your family will suggest possible solutions. Be sure to arrange a written agreement with a family member as you would with a stranger. If you were to become unhappy with the arrangement, think about how difficult it would be to ask a family member to leave your home.

Particularly if you live alone, you may enjoy sharing your home with a good friend. The companionship is an obvious benefit, and there is added security with two or more people living in a home. You also can afford more services when you pool resources and save physical energy by sharing household chores.

Making It Legal

Each arrangement has the common element of an exchange mutually beneficial to both parties. Clearly specify in legal documents the terms of your agreement, including the responsibilities and obligations of each party. Include plans for settling disagreements and dissolving the agreement if the arrangement fails. Do not presume that a handshake is sufficient for an agreement with a friend or family member. A written agreement will help preserve your relationship if a controversy arises.

By renting your home, you could receive money, companionship, house maintenance, transportation, security, personal services, housekeeping, or a combination of these. If you rent for money, specify the amount and the timing of payments. If you rent for services provided or a combination of services and money, specify the time, quality, and quantity of services you expect to receive.

Exchange of services for shelter falls into a commonly used financial gray area known as barter. According to current tax law, you must include in your income, at the time received, the fair market value of services you receive in bartering. Consult your tax adviser before you rent your home or commit to any exchange of service arrangement.

Reverse Mortgages

If you own a home, you may find yourself in the unusual position of being house-rich and cash-poor. You may have considerable wealth invested in your home, but you cannot pay your bills, particularly major ones for long-term care. A reverse mortgage allows you to use the money invested in your home without selling your house or moving out of it.

Equity is the difference between the amount of money you owe on your mortgage and the market value of your house. If you have paid off your mortgage, the entire market value is your equity. For example, if you own your home outright (paid off the mortgage) and your house can be sold for $120,000, then the amount of equity you have in your home is $120,000. If you still owe a portion of your mortgage, the equity in your home is the market value ($120,000) minus the amount of mortgage remaining.

A reverse mortgage is a relatively new way to convert your equity into cash without selling or making regular repayments. It is a loan based upon the money (equity) you have in your home. The loan does not have to be repaid as long as you live in your home. You can use the money loaned to you for many different purposes such as paying off debts, supplementing your monthly income, making home repairs, or paying for health care needs.

Payments from a reverse mortgage can be in the form of a single lump sum of cash, regular monthly advances, or a line of credit. With a line of credit, you have a personal account that you can draw against up to a set value established in the mortgage agreement. Many reverse mortgages today allow you to combine forms of loan payments to you.

The loan periods for reverse mortgages can vary. Almost all reverse mortgages now provide a guarantee of lifetime tenancy, which means that you can stay in your house as long as you live. If you sell your home or permanently move away, the mortgage would become due. It is important that you clarify with the lender how long you are allowed to be away from your home, say for an extended trip or a stay of a few months in a nursing home. Some reverse mortgage plans allow you lifetime monthly advances regardless of where you live. Finally, some loans will pay term advances for an agreed period of time. With most term advances, the mortgage does not necessarily become payable at the end of the term. In some plans, it does, and consumers should be aware of the possible consequence.

When you take out a reverse mortgage, you still remain owner of your home. This means you continue to be responsible for maintaining the property, paying property taxes, and keeping it insured.

Reverse mortgages are available in all states and the District of Columbia. Several different plans are available, some more widely than others, according to the state you live in. Plan features can vary from state to state.

The amount of money you can get from a reverse mortgage depends on three primary factors:

1. *Your age.* The older you are at closing, the more money you will be loaned in most plans.
2. *Your equity.* The more equity you have in your home, the greater the amount the lender will let you borrow. Most plans have minimum and maximum limits on the amount of equity they will lend against.
3. *Loan costs.* Lenders charge for expenses such as start-up costs, interest, and service fees. Loan costs are also affected by other critical factors, like the types of cash advance you select and the length of your loan. Federal truth-in-lending laws require lenders to provide a total annual loan cost (TALC) rate. This is the best means of comparing the cost of different plans.

Reverse Mortgage Consumer Tips

- *One size does not fit all.* The amount of cash you can get and the real cost to you can vary by tens of thousands of dollars from one reverse mortgage plan to another.
- *Examine all options.* It pays to investigate all your choices. There are major differences among the plans. In most cases, the HECM provides the most cash at the lowest cost.
- *Compare total costs.* The total annual loan cost rate is the best way to compare the true, total cost to you of reverse mortgages. TALC rates decline over time and can vary substantially from one plan to another.
- *Credit lines are not equal.* Most borrowers prefer the line-of-credit form of payment. Credit lines offered by the different plans are not the same. The HECM credit line is the only one in which the remaining available credit grows larger every month until it is used up.

Choosing the best plan for your circumstances is critical. Differences in the terms of these plans can mean substantial variation in the amount of money you get. The Home Equity Conversion Mortgage (HECM) is federally insured through the U.S. Department of Housing and Urban Development. The HECM is available in all states. Fannie Mae has a program called Home Keeper that is available in all states. Financial Freedom Senior Funding has a Cash Account plan that is available in larger states.

Consumer Advice

A reverse mortgage is not the most appropriate solution for everyone. It is a fairly new type of loan and has some unfamiliar features. Therefore, before you enter into such an agreement, consider carefully your total financial picture and consult with your legal and financial advisers. Further, review materials available from consumer organizations that research this topic.

You also will want to discuss with those family members who are your heirs your plans to take out a reverse mortgage. A frank and open discussion on such a serious matter as this often prevents the pain of misunderstandings in the future. Also, such a discussion may turn up additional information, of which you were unaware, that may alter your decision.

Other Options

Aside from reverse mortgages, you can also use the equity in your home in other ways. Property tax deferral is available through a government program in many states. Money to pay your taxes is loaned to you and does not have to be repaid until you stop living in the house. For more information, contact your local property tax collector's office.

Similar to a property tax deferral is a deferred-payment loan, available from local government housing and community development agencies. This type of loan, usually with no interest charge, is for repairing and improving your home and does not need to be repaid until you stop living in the house. For more information, contact your local area agency on aging, city or county housing department, or community development agency.

For Your Information

AARP
601 E Street, NW
Washington, DC 20049
Phone: 800-424-3410
Web site: www.aarp.org

AARP has a consumer guide called Home Made Money. To request a free copy, ask for stock number D12894.

Financial Freedom Senior Funding Corporation
19782 MacArthur Boulevard, #100
Irvine, CA 92612
Phone: 800-500-5150
Web site: www.financialfreedom.com

National Center for Home Equity Conversion (NCHEC)
360 N. Robert Street, #403
St. Paul, MN 55101
Phone: 800-209-8085
Web site: www.reverse.org

3

Insurance Coverage for Home Health Care

Receiving long-term care in your home and community allows you to remain in your home with familiar surroundings. Federal programs and private insurance are available to help you pay for needed care at home. This chapter begins by discussing Medicare's coverage of home health care services and the conditions for coverage and also explains how private medigap policies provide supplemental coverage for the gaps in Medicare. Medicaid coverage of home health care is also briefly described.

Since many private long-term care insurance policies also help pay for long-term care services at home, this chapter focuses on the conditions for coverage under this insurance as well. For a comprehensive discussion of long-term care insurance, refer to Chapter 7.

The final section of this chapter explains assistance available through the Department of Veterans Affairs (VA).

Medicare

Americans 65 or older who qualify for Social Security retirement benefits, or those under 65 who qualify for disability insurance under Social Security or who have end-stage renal disease, are eligible for home health services under Medicare. This section explains the conditions under which Medicare will pay and the limits of Medicare coverage for skilled care services delivered to you in your home.

Conditions for Coverage

Medicare pays for home health service if you meet all four conditions listed below. Once you fail to meet one of the conditions, Medicare and your supplemental insurance will stop paying. Be aware that even when you seem to meet all conditions, Medicare will cease to pay once your rate of recovery reaches a plateau. If you feel that Medicare should pay your claims, you may appeal the denial.

To receive Medicare for home health care, these four conditions *must* all be met:

1. You are confined to your home (homebound).
2. The care you need is intermittent skilled nursing care, physical therapy, occupational therapy, or speech therapy.
3. Your physician determines that you need home health care and prescribes a home health plan of treatment for you.
4. You receive these services from a certified home health agency participating in Medicare.

Medicare Part A currently pays in full, with no required copayment, for home health care services if you meet the four conditions. If you have only Medicare Part B coverage, it covers medically necessary home health services and does not require you to pay a deductible or, with the exception of medical equipment, the usual 20 percent coinsurance.

Homebound implies a normal inability to leave home due to a medical condition being treated that restricts the ability of a person to leave his or her home except with the assistance of another individual or with the aid of a supportive device such as a wheelchair. To be homebound does not mean a person must be bedridden. Nor does it mean that a person can never leave his or her home. Infrequent, short absences from the house are permitted, for example to see a doctor or for other essential appointments.

The skilled services must be reasonable and necessary to treat your illness or condition and must be according to a plan of treatment prescribed by your doctor. Services must be provided by or under the direct supervision of a registered nurse or by a physical, occupational, or speech therapist.

Home health services must be needed on an intermittent or part-time basis. Intermittent is defined as less than 7 days per week, not to exceed 28 hours in any 1 week. Part-time service is defined as any number of days per week—up to a total of 28 hours—for less than 8 hours per day. The Medicare Part A fiscal intermediary (the private insurance company that handles claims on behalf of Medicare) may extend approval for up to 35 hours of services per week. For very short periods, Medicare may cover up to 8 hours per day, 7 days per week, for a maximum of 21 consecutive days of one or more visits per day of home health benefits.

Home health services are covered by Medicare only when services are provided by a home health agency that is certified by Medicare to participate in the program. Agencies that qualify may be a public health agency, a nonprofit agency, or a commercial organization. Call your local area agency on aging to request a list of home health agencies serving your community. Be sure the home care agency is Medicare-certified.

Services Covered

Medicare pays approved charges for skilled nursing care delivered to you in your home. Services must be reasonable and necessary to treat your illness or condition. Home health agencies directly bill Medicare Part A, or Part B if you are eligible for it and not Part A. Skilled services must be performed by or under the direct supervision of a registered nurse. The need for nursing care is based on the complexity of services and your condition. A service is not necessarily "skilled" just because it is performed by a registered nurse, nor is a service "unskilled" because it is performed by someone other than a registered nurse.

> ### Home Care Services Medicare Covers
>
> - Skilled nursing
> - Physical therapy
> - Speech therapy
> - Occupational therapy*
> - Medical social services†
> - Home health aide services†
>
> *Covered only if part of a plan that includes skilled nursing care, physical therapy, or speech therapy.
>
> †Covered only if part of a plan that includes skilled services.

If Medicare covers your skilled nursing care, physical therapy, occupational therapy, or speech therapy, Medicare may also pay for services for a home health aide or a medical social worker. These services must be prescribed in your physician's treatment plan and provided at the same time as the skilled care. If you are not receiving skilled services, Medicare will not pay for these additional services.

Home health aides provide primarily personal care services, which include bathing, skin care, hair care, care of teeth, assistance with oral medication, and assistance with movement. A home health aide may also help with meal preparation, light housekeeping, laundry, or dishwashing as long as these services are incidental to the personal care provided. These nonpersonal care services are otherwise not covered by Medicare.

Medicare does not cover custodial care in the home. Custodial care implies services that are primarily for the purpose of meeting personal needs and that are provided by persons without medical training or professional skills. Services provided by a home health aide are primarily custodial services and are not covered except in conjunction with skilled care administered at the same time.

Home health agencies may offer the services of a home care aide, companion, or homemaker. Usually these services are provided on an hourly basis, but you may contract for longer periods of time. As Medicare does not cover these services unless they are given at the same time as skilled services, you must pay privately for these services yourself.

Often special equipment will allow you to live comfortably in your home without having to move into a nursing home. Equipment such as wheelchairs, hospital beds, and oxygen pumps are called durable medical equipment. Medical supplies include splints and dressings. When durable medical equipment or medical supplies are prescribed by your physician and provided through a certified medical equipment supplier, Medicare pays. If equipment or supplies are provided in conjunction with Medicare-covered skilled home care, Medicare Part A pays 100 percent; otherwise Medicare Part B pays for 80 percent of approved charges.

Medicare Supplemental Insurance (Medigap Insurance)

Many older persons have a supplemental Medicare health insurance policy. These policies are designed to pay for copayments and deductibles associated with Medicare's payment for acute health care services. Medigap policies, as they are called, do not pay for home health care unless Medicare approves the service and pays for some portion. If Medicare does not cover a service, your medigap policy will not cover it either.

Medigap policies vary considerably. Carefully read your medigap policy to be sure you know what home health services are covered and under what conditions. Among the ten standardized medigap plans, four plans (D, G, I, and J) provide an at-home recovery benefit. This benefit pays for personal care services when Medicare covers skilled home health care after an illness or injury. Personal care includes help with activities of daily living. To be eligible for this benefit, you must qualify for skilled home health care under Medicare. The benefit pays up to $40 per visit for no more than 7 visits per week and can be used up to 8 weeks after your Medicare-covered home health care visits stop. A total of 40 visits per year is covered, with the result that the maximum annual coverage is $1,600. For every visit you receive that is paid by Medicare, the policy will cover one personal care visit.

Medicaid

Medicaid is a joint federal-state entitlement program that helps to pay for medical services, including home health care, to low-income people. States administer the Medicaid program following broad federal standards. Consequently, qualifications for Medicaid coverage and services covered vary from state to state.

Medicaid-funded home health care services are available to individuals entitled to skilled nursing facility services. Most states pay for home health care services if they are cheaper than the cost of a nursing home. All states are required to offer the following home health services to people eligible for Medicaid: nursing, home health aides, and medical supplies and equipment used in the home. States have the option of covering physical, occupational, and speech therapy as home care services. States can also choose to cover other home health care services such as homemaker or chore services, personal care, and respite care. In the current era of welfare reform and tight government budgets, the support of some states for home care services may diminish in the future.

The financial criteria for Medicaid eligibility are complicated and vary from state to state. For more about these criteria as well as for additional general information about Medicaid, refer to Chapter 6.

Long-Term Care Insurance

Most long-term care insurance policies offered today will automatically include home care. With older policies, however, home care coverage is a separate option or a rider to a policy covering nursing home care. Older policies should be reviewed to determine if they provide home care or not. Most policies issued, even as recently as 10 years ago, did not offer home care and often required hospitalization prior to payment of benefits. Policies differ on the conditions to qualify for coverage, the amount paid, the number of home care visits covered, and the services the policy will cover. Be certain that you fully understand either your existing policy or one that is being offered to you.

Conditions for Coverage

Policies differ on the conditions required to qualify for home care benefits. Older policies require a prior hospital stay or a specified period of time in a nursing home, such as 31 days, in order to qualify for home care benefits. As these older policies often do not cover personal care services, most people agree that such policies do not provide effective coverage for home care. Newer policies do, however.

Some older policies require that a physician certify that the home care is medically necessary or is needed because of an illness or injury. Tax-qualified policies require a health care practitioner to prescribe a plan of care for home care. While many people need home care because of an acute medical problem, many others need home care for chronic problems or frailty.

Many newer policies require that you meet one of two conditions. Either you have a physical impairment, defined as being unable to perform activities of daily living without the assistance of another person, or you have a cognitive impairment, defined as a diminished mental capacity. This is a valuable feature in a policy since it will cover people with chronic problems, people who simply need help because of getting older, or people with Alzheimer's disease.

Services Covered

Most policies cover skilled, intermediate, and custodial care at home. Coverage for skilled home care is normally not needed in a long-term care policy because Medicare pays for certain amounts of it. However, a long-term care policy should cover custodial or personal care services.

The few policies that cover custodial care only if it is in conjunction with skilled care really do not have home care coverage. An effective home care benefit would cover home care aides and personal assistants, as well as the skilled providers such as an RN, an LPN, and therapists. Many policies cover an adult day health care center; a few cover adult day centers that do not provide therapeutic services. Many policies cover a maximum of 14 to 30 or more days of respite care, defined as the temporary care that relieves the caregiver.

Some policies require that you receive home care from a home care agency. This may be restrictive. Home care agencies do a very good job at providing skilled care at home. However, there can be chronic problems with personal assistants and home care aides. They may not arrive on time, or at all. You may have to work with a different person each time. Look for home care coverage that provides the most flexibility in coverage.

Most policies cover assisted living facilities as institutional care, and as such, the daily maximum is the same for both nursing homes and assisted living facilities, or at least the reimbursement level for the assisted living facility keys off the nursing home maximum. Be aware, however, that some policies give assisted living facilities a daily maximum that equals the home care daily maximum, even though the coverage resides in the institutional portion of the policy. Policies now pay for room and board charges, as well as personal care services, under the daily maximum allowance.

Amount of Coverage

Benefits under some policies are often dependent on the amount paid for nursing home care. This could be as low as 50 percent or as high as 100 percent of the benefit for nursing home care. Some policies allow you to decide the home care benefit amount independently from the benefit amount for nursing home care. Read your policy or proposal carefully.

Part-time home care, such as a 3- to 4-hour visit per day, should cost less than nursing home care. A policy paying 50 percent of nursing home benefits may be adequate for part-time home care services. However, you will probably need a primary caregiver in order to receive effective part-time home care service. Without a primary caregiver, you probably need a policy that pays home care at the same rate as nursing home care because you will need more extensive home care services.

Another restriction is the number of home health visits the policy will cover. Older policies differ on the definition of maximum number of visits. Some policies state a maximum number. Others vary the number of visits according to the number of days you are confined to the nursing home; the longer the confinement, the more home visits covered. Newer policies stipulate a maximum lifetime amount of benefits, typically 2 or more years of long-term care. If your policy pays 50 percent of the benefit amount for home care, you should look for a policy that considers the maximum dollar benefit. A 2-year policy will cover 4 years of home care paying at 50 percent.

Long-term care policies that cover home care can certainly help you pay for home care expenses. Read the policy carefully to understand the coverage before you purchase the insurance and inform family members about the coverage. For a comprehensive discussion of long-term care insurance coverage, refer to Chapter 7.

Veterans' Benefits

The Veterans Health Care Eligibility Reform Act of 1996 requires that after October 1, 1998, a veteran must be enrolled to receive VA health care services, with a few exceptions. The law also removes previous differences in a veteran's eligibility for inpatient and outpatient services. Needed hospital and medical services can now generally be provided in the most clinically appropriate settings for enrolled veterans in need of VA care.

The uniform benefits package available to all enrolled veterans includes inpatient hospital care; ambulatory care; emergency care (in VA facilities); rehabilitative, home health, respite, and hospice care; medically necessary drugs, pharmaceuticals, and durable medical equipment; and adult day health care.

The Department of Veterans Affairs may provide nursing home care in VA facilities when medically indicated and to the extent resources and facilities are available to both service- and nonservice-connected veterans. Certain nonservice-connected and zero percent service-connected veterans with higher income levels are required to make copayments for their care. Veterans who have been furnished hospital, nursing home, or domiciliary care in VA facilities may be transferred to community nursing homes at VA expense. Under this contract program, nursing home care at VA expense for nonservice-connected veterans is limited to a period of time not to exceed 6 months following hospitalization in a VA facility. Contract care for veterans who received hospital care for a service-connected disability is not subject to the 6-month limit. The State Home per Diem Program, a grant-in-aid program, allows the VA to pay states an established per diem rate that covers up to half the cost of care for eligible veterans in VA-recognized state nursing homes. States may set additional eligibility standards, such as residency requirements.

For the most up-to-date information about benefits and your eligibility, contact your local VA office or medical facility.

For Your Information

Centers for Medicare and Medicaid Services (CMS)
(formerly known as the Health Care Financing Administration)
7500 Security Boulevard
Baltimore, MD 21244-1850
Phone: 800-633-4227
Web sites: www.hcfa.gov and www.cms.gov

CMS manages the Medicare and Medicaid programs, operates a telephone hot line, and publishes the *Medicare Handbook* and *Guide to Health Insurance for People on Medicare*. To obtain a free copy of either book or of several other pamphlets including one on Medicare's coverage of home care, call the toll-free number above.

Department of Veterans Affairs (VA)
810 Vermont Avenue, NW
Washington, DC 20420
Phone: 800-827-1000
Web site: www.va.gov

The VA provides a variety of federal benefits to veterans of military service and their dependents. Eligibility depends upon individual circumstances.

National Association for Home Care (NAHC)
228 Seventh Street, SE
Washington, DC 20003
Phone: 202-547-7424
Web site: www.nahc.org

NAHC is a professional organization that represents a variety of agencies providing home care services. Write or go online for a list of available materials.

Paralyzed Veterans of America (PVA)
Veterans Benefits Department
801 18th Street, NW
Washington, DC 20006
Phone: 800-424-8200 (in Washington, DC: 872-1300)
Web site: www.pva.org

PVA is a veterans service organization chartered by Congress to provide benefits, counseling, and claims representation for all veterans. These services are free of charge.

4

Supportive Living Arrangements

Not everyone chooses to continue living in his or her home. You may want less space or less maintenance, tighter security, assistance in caring for yourself, or companionship.

Supportive living is a broad term that refers to living accommodations with built-in long-term care services. In some arrangements, the degree of independence is the same as living in your own home, but with long-term care services readily available. Supportive living arrangements provide a physical and social environment that contributes to a resident's continued intellectual, psychological, and physical growth.

Shared Living

Shared living offers housing arrangements that provide private living space and common facilities, such as meeting rooms, recreation facilities, and dining areas, that are shared by residents. Living spaces may be private apartments or bedrooms. Shared living facilities are developed by corporations, individuals, and nonprofit groups. In most communities, these living arrangements are licensed by health or social service agencies. The nature and extent of regulations governing the operations of shared living facilities vary widely from state to state.

Shared living arrangements are available under several different names and forms. Adult foster care is a single-family home that provides a residence for unrelated older persons unable to function independently. Congregate housing is multiunit rental housing, usually with support services such as meals, housekeeping, and social and recreational activities. Personal care housing is group living that provides nonmedical services such as meals, housekeeping, and personal care. Other names for personal care housing are group home, board-and-care home, assisted living, or domiciliary care. A retirement home or a retirement community is an independent living accommodation for persons who prefer to live independently, but in a safe, structured environment.

The purpose of shared living arrangements is to allow you to continue to live as independently as possible for as long as possible. Costs vary by the type and size of accommodation you choose and by the extent of services offered. Many shared living arrangements offer comprehensive services short of medical or nursing care. Often all or some meals and housekeeping services are provided. The emphasis on assistance with personal care and other supervision is the difference between a personal care facility and an adult congregate living facility.

Assisted Living

Assisted living is one of the fastest-growing types of shared living arrangements for older persons. Assisted living facilities provide a combination of housing and personalized care in a professionally managed group living setting with a homelike environment. Facilities may range from detached houses and cottages in a campuslike setting to full apartments with complete kitchens, as well as single rooms without kitchens. Some facilities have special units to accommodate people with the early stages of Alzheimer's disease. In return for a monthly fee, residents may receive, in addition to a place to live, at least one of an array of services that include meals, laundry and housekeeping, medication monitoring, personal care, and transportation outside the facility.

Included in the definition of assisted living are homes that serve as few as three or four people to facilities that serve several hundred residents. Some facilities provide their own standard package of services to all residents, while other facilities make services available based on a resident's needs for service and willingness and ability to pay for specific additional services.

Assisted living facilities differ from personal care homes in the emphasis on supervision and ability to offer assistance as needed rather than on a scheduled basis. Some offer comprehensive services that are just short of medical or nursing care. Geared to the more frail elderly, these services often include assistance with one or more of the activities of daily living such as bathing and dressing. If private-duty nursing is necessary, a resident usually must arrange and pay for this. If constant nursing care is needed, a resident normally must leave an assisted living facility.

The philosophy of assisted living is to allow each resident the right to make choices about his or her health and safety. Since these choices may include activities or habits that others consider risky, this philosophy accepts the fact that the resident also has the right to incur a degree of risk.

The interpretation of this philosophy varies among facilities. In considering any assisted living facility, prospective residents and their families will want to clarify the management's philosophy of assisted living.

The cost of assisted living facilities for the most part must be borne by individual residents and their families. Some long-term care insurance policies may cover aspects of care in an assisted living facility. See Chapter 7 for a full explanation of long-term care insurance.

The field of assisted living is so new that there are few standardized definitions of services and facilities, as well as few consumer guides. The Consumer Consortium on Assisted Living, a grassroots consortium of consumers, caregivers, providers, and long-term care professionals based largely in metropolitan Washington, D.C., has developed a list of questions consumers can use in selecting an assisted living facility. These questions are presented in the box "Questions to Ask When Choosing an Assisted Living Facility."

Financially Assisted Housing

The U.S. Department of Housing and Urban Development (HUD), the Federal Housing Administration (FHA), and state housing finance authorities fund housing programs for older people. Financially assisted housing is rental housing built and operated with financial help from federal,

Questions to Ask When Choosing an Assisted Living Facility*

Contracts, Costs, and Financing

What is the monthly fee? What is not included?

Can the fee change? When, how often, why? How are you involved, and what notice is given?

Does the contract clearly describe the responsibilities of the home and the resident?

Can you make changes in the contract?

What is the grievance procedure? How is a complaint filed, and to whom does it go? What if you are not satisfied with the decision? What outside agency will help?

Admission, Discharge, and Transfer

What kind of assessment is done to determine your needs? What are the qualifications of the person conducting the assessment?

What happens if your needs change—you need more help, become incontinent, become cognitively impaired, go to the hospital?

Are there limits to the amount of care you can receive?

What are reasons for discharge? Who makes the decision? What notice is given?

How does the facility assist you if you need to be discharged?

What happens if your funds run out? Is there any financial assistance? What agencies can help?

Independence and Risk

What if you want an exception to a policy, e.g., skipping breakfast, signing in and out?

What if you refuse meals or don't want to adhere to a special diet?

What if you are confused and refuse meals or medications, or want to wander the neighborhood?

What if you don't like the staff person assigned to you, or the residents at your table?

What input do you have in activity and meal planning?

continued

Services and Responsibilities

Is there a set schedule for help with such needs as bathing and dressing? Can this be changed?

How are staff scheduled to meet emergency or unplanned needs like incontinence, unexpected outings, or unanticipated problems?

Who notifies the responsible party in emergencies, when toiletries need replacement, when a status change is noted?

What is your responsibility in an emergency or when your condition changes?

What is the housekeeping schedule, and who has responsibility for your room?

What happens if there is a spill or accident that destroys property— yours or the home's? Who is responsible for cleaning, repairing, or replacement and for any costs?

Staff and Training

How many staff are there for each shift or time of day? What are their responsibilities?

Who gives the direct care? What training and certification do they have? What are the trainers' qualifications?

How many residents are assigned to each direct-care staff person? What other duties does the direct-care staff person have during these hours?

Is there any special training for staff to learn about dementia and Alzheimer's disease?

Are staff trained to deal with aggressive individuals or in behavior modification?

What kind of emergencies are staff expected to handle, and how are they trained for them?

Wellness and Health Care

Is there a nurse? What are the nurse's responsibilities and hours? Who is responsible when the nurse is not on duty?

Are there regularly scheduled visits by a nurse or other health provider? Where are records kept? Are they confidential?

continued

Is there a plan of care? How and with whom is it developed or revised? How are you involved? What involvement does a confused resident have?

What if you don't agree with your plan of care?

What health services are available in the home—lab work, physical therapy, wound care, hospice, social work, podiatrist, etc.? What does the home provide, and what can outside agencies provide?

Who gives medications? If not a nurse, how are staff trained and supervised? Who reviews medication procedures and how frequently? What are their qualifications?

How and by whom is the medication system managed?

Activities, Socializing, and Support

What kinds of activities are provided?

Who develops and supervises the activities? What is the person's background?

Are there activities outside the home? How often? How are residents transported? What staff are included?

Can you walk on the grounds? Are there accessible pathways? Are there protected or enclosed walking areas?

Can religious or spiritual needs be met? Are there services in the home or transportation to them?

Meals and Nutrition

What times are meals served?

What happens if you are late, miss a meal, or refuse a meal?

Can special diets, such as those with specific salt, calorie, or protein levels, be accommodated? If yes, who develops these? Does he or she have specific training for this?

Does a nutritionist or dietitian review meals and special diets? If yes, how often?

Safety

What kind of security system is in place for the building and personal property?

Which doors are locked and when? When doors are locked, how does one access the home? Are exit doors alarmed?

continued

Are there safety locks on the windows? If yes, what type?

Is there an emergency generator or alternate power source?

Is there a fire emergency plan? Are there fire drills? Are emergency plans publicly displayed?

Are there call bells in each room? How often are they checked to be sure they are working correctly?

Is the home layout conducive to wandering? What safety measures are in place?

Transportation

What transportation is provided by the home? How can special appointments be scheduled, and what is the cost?

Is a transportation wheelchair accessible?

What qualifications does the driver have? How are these verified?

*This list of questions was prepared by:

The Consumer Consortium on Assisted Living
PO Box 3375
Arlington, VA 22203
Phone: 703-841-2333
Web site: www.ccal.org

state, or municipal governments and designed for low-income individuals and families. Most federally assisted housing programs are structured to be sponsored and owned by nonprofit organizations. Some financially assisted housing is designed specifically for the elderly and incorporates safety, accessibility, and security features. You must meet age and income eligibility criteria. There is usually a waiting list for available housing.

Public housing consists of apartment buildings whose construction or purchase is financed through bonds sold by a public housing authority (PHA). The federal government makes annual contributions to PHAs to cover the debt service on these bonds and generally provides operating subsidies to maintain low rent for older people. Besides financial assistance, some facilities provide social and physical support. Living accommodations may include meals, housekeeping, and transportation. Social activities are often readily available to residents. Although medical care is usually not provided, a nurse or social worker is sometimes available for referral to community resources.

Continuing Care Retirement Communities

A continuing care retirement community (CCRC) combines in one convenient setting housing, health care, and social services. The basic idea of a CCRC is that as the needs of residents change, the residents can, without leaving the community, receive appropriate care across a continuum from independent living to nursing home care. Usually a resident pays an entrance fee and monthly payments to the community. In return, the CCRC agrees to provide housing and defined long-term care services for the life of the resident.

Most popular in California, Florida, Illinois, Maryland, Ohio, and Pennsylvania, CCRCs have spread to many parts of the United States during the past 15 years. Although some large corporations have developed CCRCs, the majority are established by nonprofit, mostly religious-affiliated, organizations.

Types of CCRCs

Although similar in concept, individual communities offer different contract provisions. Most communities offer a variety of contract options. Fees are structured either as refundable entry fees plus a monthly service fee (as for a condominium or rental) or as an endowment. Residency agreements are offered in three types: all inclusive, fee for service, and modified.

For an entrance fee and monthly payments, an all-inclusive continuing care contract covers housing and all long-term care services, including assistance with daily living, skilled nursing care, and custodial nursing home care. Because all services are included, the fees are higher than for other types of CCRCs. The only noninclusive services are some medical services usually covered by Medicare and supplemental health insurance that residents are generally required to maintain.

The fee-for-service community provides housing, social and recreational services, plus guaranteed access to long-term care services, including nursing home care. Generally less expensive than the all-inclusive type of CCRC, the fee-for-service community offers a different approach to providing the continuum of long-term care services.

In a fee-for-service CCRC, long-term care and medical services are the responsibility of the individual resident. None of these services is prepaid. Each resident pays for the services as they are required. The advantage is knowing that the long-term care services are available when needed. If you select a fee-for-service CCRC, you may need to consider financial arrangements to pay for needed long-term care.

A modified continuing care community is a cross between all-inclusive and the fee-for-service communities. It provides housing, social services, and physical assistance as part of the entrance and monthly fees. However, only a specified amount of nursing home care is included for the fixed fee. Additional nursing home services are available within the community for additional fees, generally lower than full costs.

The entrance fee and monthly fees of a modified CCRC are lower than those of an all-inclusive community because the expensive portion of long-term nursing home care is limited, and higher than the fees in a fee-for-service CCRC because some long-term care services are guaranteed.

Entrance and Monthly Fees

For all CCRCs, residents pay a lump-sum entrance fee when beginning their residency. Formerly when a resident died or left the community, the fee was not refundable. Now, however, many CCRCs will refund part of the entrance fee upon a variety of specified conditions. Before you sign a contract, you will want to review carefully the terms for refunds.

Entrance and monthly fees vary by the size of the unit (studio, one-bedroom, two-bedroom, or larger) and by the location and type of CCRC. A recent industry survey reports that the average entrance fees for one- and two-bedroom apartments ranged between $59,000 and $121,000. The average monthly fee for one person living in a one- or two-bedroom unit ranged between $1,000 and $1,600. Like condominium fees, monthly CCRC fees are subject to periodic increases depending on the operating costs of the complex.

The concept of a CCRC can be very appealing. Unfortunately, some people have lost money when communities collapsed financially before they could fulfill their promises. Investigate the community to be sure it is financially stable. Providing a full continuum of services is expensive. Often, communities find they are providing more expensive medical care than expected.

Reviewing the Contract

Before you sign a contract with a CCRC, carefully examine the services the community provides as part of your entrance and monthly fees, as

Continuing Care Retirement Community Worksheet

	CCRC1	CCRC 2
1. Entrance fee		
How much?	_____	_____
Is the entrance fee refundable?	_____	_____
What is the refund policy?	_____	_____
2. Monthly fee		
Accommodations:		
Studio	_____	_____
One bedroom	_____	_____
Two bedrooms	_____	_____
Other	_____	_____
3. If spouse enters nursing home, do accommodations change?	_____	_____
4. Can monthly fee increase?	_____	_____
Conditions for increases	_____	_____
5. Long-term care services		
Assisted living (If not covered, how much?)	_____	_____
Skilled care	_____	_____
Personal care	_____	_____
Nursing home (If not covered, how much?)	_____	_____
Skilled	_____	_____
Intermediate	_____	_____
Custodial	_____	_____
Any restrictions?	_____	_____
6. Termination		
Conditions for me to terminate contract	_____	_____
Conditions for CCRC to terminate contract	_____	_____
7. What is not included in the fees?	_____	_____
8. What other expenses are expected?	_____	_____

opposed to the services for which you are expected to pay. The contract should clearly state under what conditions the community is allowed to increase or decrease monthly fees.

It is unlikely that a contract will include a clause to terminate it. But if it does, the terms and procedures for the termination should be clearly stated. Also, review the procedures for adjusting monthly fees when you change your living accommodations. If you move to the nursing facility, the contract should state how long your living quarters are maintained during a nursing stay and the conditions under which a spouse stays in the living quarters while the other spouse is in the nursing quarters.

Reviewing a CCRC contract requires legal and financial assistance, and more importantly, some frank discussions about the rest of your life.

For Your Information

American Association of Homes and Services for the Aging (AAHSA)
2519 Connecticut Avenue, NW
Washington, DC 20008
Phone: 800-508-9442
Web site: www.aahsa.org

AAHSA is a national association of nonprofit organizations dedicated to providing quality housing, health, community, and related services to older people. Among its publications for consumers is a free brochure on assisted living.

Assisted Living Federation of America (ALFA)
11200 Waples Mill Road, Suite 150
Fairfax, VA 22030
Phone: 703-691-8100
Web site: www.alfa.org

ALFA is a national nonprofit membership organization dedicated to enhancing the quality of life in assisted living residences and promoting the interests of the assisted living industry. It has published a checklist to help assess the important services, amenities, and accommodations in assisted living communities. For a free copy, send a stamped, self-addressed legal-size envelope.

National Center for Assisted Living (NCAL)
1201 L Street, NW
Washington, DC 20005
Phone: 202-842-4444
Web site: www.ahca.org

NCAL is the assisted living arm of the American Health Care Association representing assisted living facilities. It provides a free pamphlet on choosing an assisted living facility.

National Consumers League
1701 K Street, NW, Suite 1200
Washington, DC 20006
Phone: 202-835-3323
Web site: www.natlconsumersleague.org

The League is a nonprofit organization that works to educate consumers about many issues. It publishes a booklet about life care/continuing care retirement communities. Write or go online for a price list and ordering information.

Part II

Planning Ahead for Nursing Home Care

If you have known someone who spent some time in a nursing home, you probably feel that you want to avoid ever having to be in one yourself. Unfortunately, like most of the people in nursing homes today, you may not have a choice. Nursing homes provide medical care, supervision, and personal care for people whose condition cannot be adequately treated at home or who are unable to care for themselves and do not have someone who is able and willing to care for them at home.

People of all ages live in nursing homes. In 1998, an American Health Care Association publication estimated that 5.8 percent of all persons aged 65 and over were living in a nursing home. About 10 percent of the nursing home population is under 65 years of age. Of the 90 percent over age 65, the large majority are over age 80. The average nursing home resident is an 80-year-old white widow with several chronic conditions. As our society continues to live longer, more people will need the care and services of a nursing home. In general, people over 80 have a greater level of chronic disability, are at greater risk of suffering cognitive problems, and tend to lack a family member to help with home care. These factors contribute to the increasing chance of needing nursing home care.

Nursing homes are changing. As hospitals have provided more high-technology acute care in the past 15 years, hospital costs have escalated. To reduce the amount of money the federal government spends on hospital care, Medicare uses a reimbursement system to hospitals based on diagnosis-related groups (DRGs). The government pays the hospital an average cost of care for a patient based on the medical condition and surgery needed. If the hospital treats the patient for less, the hospital profits. This gives hospitals the incentive to shorten hospital stays.

Although many people do not need the high technology of an acute care hospital, they do need nursing care. Therefore, hospitals discharge patients to nursing homes for recuperation. Roughly 45 percent of the people admitted to a nursing home stay less than 3 months and require mostly skilled care.

The definition and composition of a nursing home are likely to change in the future. Today, nursing homes contain people with different levels and kinds of impairments. As hospitals continue to discharge patients who need nursing care, nursing homes will become more and more subacute care facilities. As more and more people suffer from Alzheimer's disease, facilities will specialize to provide the care and treatment needed by Alzheimer's patients. People needing primarily personal assistance because of physical impairments prefer to live in an assisted living facility instead of a nursing home that provides mostly subacute care. In most states assisted living facilities are not considered nursing homes. However, the subtle distinction is often lost on the public. People who sell their houses or leave their apartments to move into an assisted living facility in order to receive the services can feel that they are going to a nursing home. For more about assisted living, see Chapter 4.

A 1999 guide published by the National Association of Insurance Commissioners reported the probability of a 65-year-old person needing nursing home care. At age 65, you have a 43 percent probability of being admitted to a nursing home at some time in your lifetime. A 65-year-old woman has a 50 percent lifetime probability of entering a nursing home, but a man only a 36 percent probability. Most nursing home stays are short, recuperative stays. You have only a 24 percent probability of staying more than a year, and approximately a 9 percent probability of spending more than 5 years in a nursing home. The study shows that these probabilities increase as you grow older.

Nursing home care is expensive. In 2000, the MetLife Mature Market Institute reported that the national average cost of a private room in a nursing home was $153 a day, or $55,000 a year. Assisted living facilities generally cost approximately 30 percent less according to the Assisted Living Federation of America.

How to pay for this care is a major concern for all of us. Nursing home expenditures currently amount to approximately $70 billion per year. As shown in the accompanying graph, Medicaid pays for almost half of all nursing home costs, while private individuals and older people and their families pay about one-third.

These facts are reasons why everyone is concerned about the possibility of needing nursing home care. Ignoring the problem will not make it go away. The earlier you start planning for nursing home care, the more options are available to you.

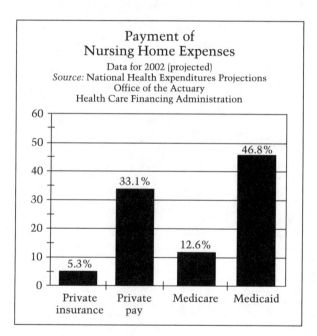

Part I of this guide presented options to remain in your home as long as possible. However, even taking advantage of all these options, you may still require assisted living or nursing home care.

Part II discusses options you have regarding individual nursing homes other than one connected with a continuing care retirement community discussed in Chapter 4. Most of this part describes current payment sources for nursing home care and other options you have to cover this expenditure.

5

Nursing Home Options Today

Nursing home care is a comprehensive and expensive service. Instead of remaining in a hospital, people often are admitted for short stays in a nursing home for recuperation and rehabilitation. Although only a small percentage of older people ever need nursing home care for an extended period of time, the prospect of needing and paying for nursing home care is a major concern of most older persons.

Nursing home care is received in a facility that may be attached to or affiliated with other health care facilities such as a clinic or hospital. States regulate the nursing home industry, requiring special certificates of need to build a facility and licensing the facility to ensure that safety codes are enforced and quality care is provided. Medicare also certifies nursing homes and will only pay for care received in a Medicare-certified facility. Many private insurers will pay only for care received in nursing homes licensed by the state. Some require that the facility also be certified by Medicare.

Your doctor is the best person to help you determine what type of care you need—skilled, intermediate, or custodial:

- Skilled care is the highest level of care and the most expensive, although only 5 percent of nursing home residents require skilled care. Medicare will pay for skilled care, but only under certain conditions and only for a short duration. Refer to Chapter 6 for information on Medicare's conditions to pay for skilled care in a nursing home.
- Intermediate care provides basic medical procedures such as those needed by some stroke victims. Medicare and your supplemental insurance policy do not pay for intermediate care. However, Medicaid and many long-term care policies pay for it.
- Custodial care is not medical care and is usually provided for people who need assistance with daily living. Medicare and supplemental insurance policies do not pay for any of the cost of custodial care. Medicaid and most long-term care insurance policies do pay for it.

Not all institutional long-term care is provided in nursing homes, and not all nursing homes are the same. States differ on the definition and licensure of nursing homes. A facility considered a nursing home in one state may not be in another state. Assisted living facilities and other primarily custodial nursing homes are the facilities that often vary from state to state. They are also called domiciliary care or personal care facilities and provide only custodial care. They usually do not provide any nursing care, but often will have a registered nurse on staff or on call. Many people consider these facilities nursing homes because they provide institutional care at a location other than at home or in the community.

Often you cannot tell by the name or marketing information the distinctions among long-term care facilities. After you have an understanding of your long-term care needs, select a place that meets them. If you need assistance with activities of daily living, you may prefer to live in an assisted living facility rather than a nursing home where people often are frail or ill. The cost of an assisted living facility is generally less than that of a nursing facility. However, if you later need nursing care, you will have to transfer to a nursing facility.

The two basic types of nursing facilities are skilled nursing facilities (SNFs) and intermediate care facilities (ICFs). The nursing home reform legislation of 1987 eliminated the distinction between skilled and intermediate-care facilities, classifying both as a nursing facility. However, since some facilities still cling to the terminology, the differences are discussed in the following paragraphs.

Most SNFs deliver intermediate and custodial as well as skilled care. In the case of skilled care, registered nurses provide 24-hour nursing services prescribed by the patient's physician. Emphasis is on medical care with restorative, physical, and occupational therapy.

An ICF delivers intermediate and custodial, but not skilled, care. The staff provides medical, social, and rehabilitative services to people in need of assistance. Less intensive nursing care is provided by registered and practical nurses on staff at the ICF.

Medicaid pays almost half of all nursing home costs in the United States. However, because of Medicaid requirements, reimbursement does not begin until a person has met the state's income and assets limits. In many instances, in order to meet these guidelines, people must deplete most of their savings and assets. Although many people begin their nursing home stay as private-pay patients, they become eligible for Medicaid when they exhaust their financial resources. Refer to Chapter 6 for more information on eligibility requirements for and coverage from Medicaid.

Choosing a Nursing Home in Advance

The first step is to learn about nursing homes in the area in which you choose to live. After you narrow the list to several homes, make a visit to each with your significant other, spouse, and/or your grown children. This will help you make the transition should you need the support of the facility. Valuable insight is learned by talking with residents of the home and with their family members.

When you tour the facility, observe the interaction of the staff with the patients and how quickly the staff responds to call signals. Check how pleasant the surroundings are and what activities are available for the residents. If you have special needs, ask if those services are available.

Once you find a facility with which you are comfortable, ask about costs and services. Based on this information, you may be able to adjust your financial resources to suit your future needs. If you choose a home that is more expensive than you had planned, you have the time to find a different facility or to arrange additional financing. A hasty and ill-conceived last-minute decision can bring financial hardship and emotional stress to your whole family.

Many good nursing homes have long waiting lists. If a home you like has a waiting list, ask that your name be added to the list. If your turn comes and you are not ready to move in, you may defer to the next person on the list.

If the need is immediate, talk to your physician, a social worker at your local area agency on aging, or a discharge planner at your community hospital. These people are available to discuss your nursing home needs and may direct you to nursing homes in your area that have available beds.

Hospice Care

Hospice care is limited to terminally ill patients. Although, as defined by this guide, hospice is not a long-term care service, it is briefly discussed here as an option for people with special needs.

Hospices strive to keep patients pain-free, comfortable, and alert during the remaining days of life and to support the family as necessary during this difficult time. Hospice care is usually provided in the home, although it can be provided in another setting such as a hospital or nursing home. You may also find a freestanding hospice unit, although they are not common in this country.

Medicare will pay the cost of hospice services, except room and board when an inpatient. The hospice continues to provide services as long as needed. Medicare will continue to pay if a physician certifies the patient's condition and need for hospice care.

To qualify for Medicare coverage of hospice care, the patient must waive his or her right to the standard Medicare coverage. This means that Medicare will not pay for an additional medical treatment for the specific medical condition. This decision is reversible,

> ### Requirements for Medicare Coverage of Hospice
>
> - Two physicians must certify that the patient has 6 months or less to live.
> - The patient must elect to receive hospice care instead of standard Medicare medical benefits for the terminal illness.
> - Hospice care must be provided by a Medicare-certified program.
> - The patient must be eligible for Medicare Part A benefits.

but no individual can have both types of coverage. Medicare will pay for treatment of unrelated medical conditions.

Hospice care provided under Medicare includes the services of doctors, nurses, social workers, therapists, home health aides, and bereavement counselors as needed and requested by the patient and family. Hospice philosophy establishes a patient-directed team. Medicare pays the hospice for your hospice care. You will have to pay:

No more than $5 for each prescription drug and other similar products. The hospice can charge up to $5 for each prescription for outpatient drugs or other similar products for pain relief and symptom control.

Five percent of the Medicare payment amount for inpatient respite care. For example, if Medicare pays $100 per day for inpatient respite care, you will pay $5 per day. You can stay in a Medicare-approved hospital or nursing care home up to 5 days each time you get respite care.

For Your Information

American Association of Homes and Services for the Aging (AAHSA)
2519 Connecticut Avenue, NW
Washington, DC 20008
Phone: 800-508-9442
Web site: www.aahsa.org

AAHSA is a national association of nonprofit organizations dedicated to providing quality housing, health, community, and related services to older people. Write, call, or go online for a free brochure on choosing a nursing home and a catalog of AAHSA's other publications.

American Health Care Association (AHCA)
1201 L Street, NW
Washington, DC 20005
Phone: 202-842-4444
Web site: www.ahca.org

AHCA represents licensed nursing homes, assisted living, and subacute care facilities. It publishes free materials on topics related to long-term care including choosing a nursing home.

Centers for Medicare and Medicaid Services (CMS)
7500 Security Boulevard
Baltimore, MD 21244
Phone: 800-633-4227
Web site: www.medicare.gov

CMS is the federal agency that manages the Medicare and Medicaid programs and has a free pamphlet titled "Guide to Choosing a Nursing Home."

National Hospice and Palliative Care Organization (NHPCO)
1700 Diagonal Road, Suite 300
Alexandria, VA 22314
Phone: 800-658-8898
Web site: www.nhpco.org

Individuals can contact NHPCO to learn about hospice service in their area and to obtain a free brochure on the topic.

6

Government Programs to Pay for Nursing Home Care

Two government programs can help you pay for health care expenses. Medicare is the federal government program intended to pay for acute medical care for people 65 years or older. Medicaid is a federal-state program designed to assist people of all ages who are unable to pay health care expenses. This chapter explains what Medicare and Medicaid pay toward nursing home care and the conditions under which these programs will pay.

Two additional programs to help you with nursing home care include the assistance provided through the Older Americans Act and Department of Veterans Affairs. This chapter also briefly explains these programs.

Aside from these programs, the federal government passed a law that promises benefit for some taxpayers. If you itemize deductions on your income tax, you can count as a medical deduction unreimbursed expenses for qualified long-term care services provided to a chronically ill person. These services include medical as well as "maintenance or personal care services" prescribed by a licensed health care practitioner. Until an interpretation of the new law is worked out in regulations, the full range of circumstances to which the law applies is not entirely clear. For up-to-date information you should check with a tax adviser.

Medicare's Limited Coverage

Many people mistakenly believe that Medicare covers the cost of your long-term care in a nursing home. In fact, Medicare pays for just a limited amount of skilled care in a nursing home under specified conditions. Medicare's main purpose is to pay for acute medical care of people 65 years and older and of younger people receiving disability benefits or with end-stage renal disease.

Conditions for Coverage

In order to be eligible for Medicare payment, you first have to be in the hospital for 3 consecutive days (not counting the day you are discharged). You must be admitted to a nursing home for a condition treated in the hospital within 30 days of leaving the hospital, and must also require skilled care in the nursing home. Medicare pays solely for skilled nursing services and rehabilitative therapy.

To qualify for continued Medicare coverage, you must need skilled nursing or rehabilitative services on a daily basis. If skilled rehabilitative services are not available 7 days a week, then receiving these services 5 days a week qualifies for the daily basis requirement. A skilled service is defined as a service that must be furnished by or under the supervision of a registered nurse and under the direction of a physician to assure safety and achieve desired medical results.

Conditions for Medicare Coverage of Nursing Home Care

- You must have a prior stay of at least 3 consecutive days (not counting the day of discharge) and be admitted to the nursing home within 30 days of discharge for the same medical condition treated in the hospital.
- You must require daily skilled nursing or rehabilitative services as prescribed by your physician in a plan of care.
- The skilled nursing facility must be Medicare-certified.

Observation and monitoring of a medically unstable condition is considered a skilled service if it requires the skills of a registered nurse to detect and evaluate a patient's need for possible modification of treatment. The attending physician must write specific orders for this service.

Medicare also covers the skilled services of physical and occupational therapists and speech pathologists. These services must be prescribed by your physician in the plan of care.

Medicare pays for services provided in a Medicare-certified skilled nursing facility. You should ask the hospital discharge planner to find a bed in such a nursing home. You should also verify certification with the nursing home administrator. Many skilled nursing facilities also offer intermediate and custodial care. This care is not covered by Medicare even though you may be in a skilled nursing facility.

Medicare Benefits

If you qualify to receive Medicare payment for nursing home care, Medicare will pay a limited amount for a limited time period. Total Medicare payment differs according to the skilled services required for care. Medicare determines payment according to the national average daily rate for care in a skilled nursing facility.

Medicare pays for 100 percent of the covered services for the first 20 days in the nursing home and for days 21 to 100 all covered services after a copayment of $101.50 per day in 2002. Medicare pays nothing after 100 days.

There is no guarantee that Medicare will pay for the full 100 days. As soon as your progress is stabilized and no further significant improvement of your condition is expected, Medicare coverage stops. This may be the sixth day or the sixtieth day after a nursing home admission. The average length of Medicare-covered nursing home services is 28 days.

Medicare Payment for Skilled Nursing Home Care

Time period	Medicare pays	You pay
Days 1–20	100% of covered service	Only for noncovered service
Days 21–100	All covered services after copayment	$101.50/day (2002) copayment plus any noncovered service
Days 101...	$0	100%

After Medicare Part A stops paying because of the time limit, Medicare Part B, if you have it, pays for specialized rehabilitative services delivered within a skilled nursing facility by speech language pathologists and audiologists, physical therapists, and occupational therapists.

As you can see, you need to make other plans to pay for any long-term care in a nursing home. Intended to pay for acute care, Medicare covers only a limited amount of skilled care in a nursing home. Medicare does not pay for any custodial care in a nursing home.

Medicare Supplemental Insurance (Medigap Insurance)

Supplemental Medicare health insurance policies are designed to pay the copayments and deductibles associated with Medicare's payment for acute health care services. Most medigap policies (plans labeled C–J) pay the copayment for days 21 to 100 in a skilled nursing facility. No medigap policies pay for long-term nursing home care. As soon as Medicare stops paying for nursing home service, your standardized medigap policy will stop. It is possible that some older nonstandardized policies will continue to pay for limited skilled care beyond Medicare's 100-day maximum.

Before you need nursing home care, carefully read your medigap policy. Policies differ, and you want to be sure you know what your policy covers and under what conditions.

Medicaid—Payer of Last Resort

Medicaid pays for almost half of nursing home care costs in the United States. It is often called the payer of last resort because it benefits only those who cannot afford to pay themselves. Under Medicaid, states must provide necessary and compassionate services to those citizens who are blind, disabled, or aged. In many states, Medicaid is available for persons falling within certain income and asset limits; not all states have spend-downs.

Medicaid is a joint federal-state entitlement program. States administer the program following broad federal standards. Each state regulates eligibility criteria, application procedures, and services covered. This guide presents in broad terms the federal guidelines for the Medicaid program. Regulations are rather complicated, and state rules vary widely. To learn the specific regulations in your state, call your local area agency on aging or your medical assistance department, or consult with an attorney familiar with this subject.

Attitudes about Medicaid vary among consumers. Some people consider Medicaid a welfare program and something to avoid at all costs. Other people recognize that they have helped to support the funding of Medicaid with their tax dollars and it is in fact something they are entitled to on the basis of medical and financial need.

Medicaid is a godsend for many families faced with overwhelming nursing home bills. To be eligible, however, you must meet rather strict financial limitations. This can mean that you will first need to exhaust most of your financial assets. In many states, a single person needs to spend down to as little as $2,000 in assets. You are also allowed $1,500 for a burial fund. In about half of the states, you are eligible for Medicaid as soon as your assets are spent. A number of states also require people to qualify on income. If you have income over your state's cap, you will not qualify for Medicaid in this state even if you have spent all your assets. Federal regulations, however, now allow people with income exceeding the cap to qualify for Medicaid by putting their income into a special trust (qualified income trust, sometimes called Miller trust). Upon the nursing home resident's death, any funds remaining in the trust must be used to reimburse the state for the amount of Medicaid assistance.

Many states also extend Medicaid benefits to people whose income is slightly above the eligibility level set by their state. These persons are called "medically needy." They are allowed to spend down their "excess" income by paying or incurring medical expenses not reimbursed by insurance, such as deductibles and copayments, or by paying premiums for Medicare Part B and medigap policies.

When a married couple spends down its resources so that one spouse is eligible for Medicaid assistance for nursing home care, the other "community" spouse could theoretically become impoverished. To prevent this from happening, a married couple is allowed to protect some assets and income for use by the spouse who remains in the community. The amount protected, called the Medicaid spousal impoverishment limit, is higher than allowed for the institutionalized spouse and is adjusted for inflation each year.

The Medicaid asset limit protected for the community spouse is one-half of all assets in either or both spouses' names. Federal guidelines set a guaranteed minimum amount that must be protected and also set a protected maximum. Certain assets, called exempt assets, are not calculated in the guaranteed and maximum amounts. These exempt assets include your principal residence, personal belongings, one car, and a $1,500 burial account for each person. The guaranteed minimum resource allowance amount and the maximum total of assets allowed to be kept by the community spouse are adjusted each year. In 2002 they are $17,856 and $89,280, respectively. Most states have raised the guaranteed amount, many up to the maximum. Check with your local area agency on aging or the medical assistance department for the current Medicaid asset limit in your state.

If you and your spouse have assets of $175,000, excluding exempt assets, then only the maximum of $89,280 is protected in 2002. If you have assets of $100,000, then $50,000 is protected. However, if you live in a state that raised the guaranteed protected amount to the maximum, then the full $89,280 is protected. Remember these amounts are subject to annual increases.

A community spouse is allowed to retain a basic monthly income allowance up to 150 percent of the federal poverty level for two people, plus, if applicable, an excess shelter allowance. Both cannot exceed an inflation-adjusted cap. In 2002 this is $2,232 per month. The community spouse can keep all the income in his or her own name. If the income is in the name of the spouse in the nursing home, the community spouse can take income from the nursing home spouse up to the maximum allowed.

In order for Medicaid to pay for nursing home care, the facility must be a certified Medicaid provider in the state. Further, the patient must be medically in need of the level of care provided in the nursing facility.

Once a person is on Medicaid, his or her income, if any, is primarily applied toward the Medicaid payment rate for that facility or used to supplement the community spouse's income if it is below the minimum monthly allowance. The patient may keep a very small monthly allowance for personal needs. Medicaid pays the difference between the amount of the patient's income and the Medicaid rate for that nursing home.

It is usually easier to enter a nursing home of your choice if you are a private-pay patient than if you are on Medicaid. Because the Medicaid-approved rate of payment is lower than what the nursing home charges private-pay patients, many nursing homes are reluctant to accept Medicaid patients. After you are in a nursing home, you may later qualify for Medicaid and remain at the facility. Once you are on Medicaid, the reluctance of some nursing homes to accept Medicaid patients may make it difficult for you to transfer to another facility even though discrimination is illegal.

Nursing homes are not supposed to discriminate against patients who go on Medicaid. However, some states do allow Medicaid patients to be assigned to a separate wing of the nursing home, or to be discharged to another nursing home if no Medicaid bed is available. If while on Medicaid you have to receive acute care in a hospital, the nursing home will keep your Medicaid bed for you for a limited time. If this period expires, the nursing home may not readmit you.

Financial Eligibility

Although financial criteria for eligibility are different for each state's Medicaid program, all programs require income and asset limits. If husband and wife live together, the combined nonexempted assets are considered when determining Medicaid eligibility. If one spouse is already in a nursing home, income is based on whose income it is. The financial status of other family members, such as children or brothers and sisters, is not included in the eligibility determination.

Meeting the asset limit is the most difficult criterion when applying for Medicaid. Exempt from asset limits are household goods, personal effects, one automobile, burial plots, $1,500 in funds for burial expenses, life insurance policies with a face value of $1,500 or less, and property-producing income that can be used to help pay for nursing home fees. In most states, the principal residence is also exempt if a spouse or dependent still lives in it or if you expect to return to it. Some states exempt the home for a specified period of time or require a physician's certification that you expect to return home.

All states are required to recover from the estates of deceased Medicaid beneficiaries the cost of care paid for by Medicaid. For most people their major asset is their home. Some states will place a lien on the property.

If you have assets above the Medicaid limit, you have two ways to qualify for Medicaid. (1) Either you must foresee the potential need for Medicaid well in advance of applying and transfer assets to other people or institutions, or otherwise legally restructure assets. Or (2) you must spend down your savings and assets, with the exception of allowable exempt resources such as your home, to the asset limit permitted in your state.

States are required to determine, at the time of application for Medicaid benefits, whether the applicant has sold or given away assets within the previous 36 months. This length of time is called the look-back period. If such a disposal occurred, states will delay eligibility for Medicaid benefits according to a mathematical formula. The number of months delayed roughly equals the amount of disallowed assets divided by the average monthly cost of nursing home care.

There are many problems in transferring assets either outright or through an irrevocable trust. Apart from whether you may have ethical considerations about this issue, an important concern is the lack of independence you will encounter after you give your assets away.

Protecting assets for a spouse is encouraged. If a spouse will need to go into a nursing home and assets have to be spent to qualify for Medicaid, the community spouse should consider using existing assets to pay off the mortgage, make home improvements, or buy a newer car since these assets are protected. This will reduce the amount of assets that have to be spent for nursing home care before Medicaid starts to pay.

Income criteria for eligibility include income from all sources. The total monthly income, less any allowable deductibles, is compared with the cost of long-term care. Once you are on Medicaid, all monthly income is signed over to Medicaid except a small personal allowance, spousal or dependent allowance, allowance to maintain a home if you are expected to return to the community, and an allowance to pay Medicare and supplemental health insurance premiums as well as medical or health services not covered by Medicaid. The amounts allowed for these deductibles differ by state programs.

In summary, you should realize three main points about Medicaid rules for financial eligibility. First, they are complicated, especially if you plan to transfer any assets. Second, the rules vary considerably from state to state. And third, in this era of welfare reform and tight government budgets, Medicaid continually faces possible changes. For all these reasons you would be wise to consult with Medicaid experts before you apply and particularly before you attempt to transfer any assets.

How, When, and Where to Apply

To apply for Medicaid, you must submit an application to your local department of social services or public assistance. A personal interview is usually required at the initial application. If the applicant is unable to apply in person, a representative may apply on his or her behalf. Assistance of an attorney familiar with elder-law issues or of someone very familiar with this process can be valuable.

When you call for an appointment, ask what information or supporting documentation is required. Generally, you should take identification such as your Social Security card, birth certificate, or immigration papers; verification of all income sources, including pensions, Social Security, rental income, interest, and dividends; verification of all assets such as bank and credit union account statements for the past 36 months, stock certificates, saving bonds, certificates of deposit, life insurance, tax bill or receipt of recent sale of home, health insurance card and statement of premium; and verification of need for nursing home care.

Additional items or verification may be required. Eligibility determination cannot be completed until all documentation and information are provided. If you are already in a nursing home, ask that your name be placed on a waiting list for available Medicaid beds and start the application process at least 3 months prior to expected need for coverage. Although, coverage can be retroactive for 3 months.

Other Government Programs

Older Americans Act

Under the Older Americans Act, your local area agency on aging is required to reach out to community residents in nursing homes. An ombudsman program encourages volunteers to regularly visit nursing home residents. In every state an ombudsman program provides supervised volunteers to encourage constructive liaisons between residents and nursing home staff. Volunteers funnel complaints from residents to the nursing home administration. Many improvements in resident comfort and services are accomplished with help from the ombudsman program.

The ombudsman program is an excellent resource to learn about nursing homes in your community. You should ask about complaint information, quality of care, or other problems discovered.

To learn more about the ombudsman program, call your local area agency on aging. You will find the telephone number in the government section of your telephone book under "Aging Services," "Department of Elder Affairs," or other similar names.

Veterans' Benefits

The Department of Veterans Affairs (VA) provides nursing home benefits but is not required to furnish them to certain categories of veterans as in the case of hospital care. Veterans with a service-connected disability are given first priority, regardless of their income level, and receive free care.

Veterans with nonservice-connected disabilities or illnesses may receive nursing home care in a VA facility if space and resources are available. A veteran with a nonservice-connected disability whose income is above an annually set level is required to pay a deductible and copayment.

Veterans with a service-connected disability are eligible to receive nursing home care in a VA facility or a private nursing home at VA expense. Direct admission to private nursing homes is limited to veterans (1) who the VA determines require nursing home care for a service-connected disability and (2) who have been discharged from a VA medical center and are receiving home health services from a VA medical center.

Skilled nursing home care authorized by the VA on a contract basis is normally limited to 6 months, except for veterans whose care relates to a service-connected disability. Veterans whose income does not exceed the maximum annual rate of the VA pension and those who the Secretary of Veterans Affairs determines have no adequate means of support are eligible to receive long-term intermediary or custodial care.

The surviving spouse or children of certain veterans are eligible to receive health care benefits. Those qualifying are the beneficiaries of veterans who (1) have a permanent and total service-connected disability, (2) died as a result of a service-connected disability or at the time of death had a total permanent service-connected disability, or (3) died while on active military duty in the line of duty.

The VA is in the process of implementing new legislation that realigns eligibility and modifies levels of services that will be provided. To obtain the most up-to-date information about these benefits and your eligibility, contact your local VA office or medical facility.

For Your Information

Department of Veterans Affairs (VA)
810 Vermont Avenue, NW
Washington, DC 20420
Phone: 800-827-1000
Web site: www.va.gov

The VA provides a variety of federal benefits available to veterans of military service and their dependents. Eligibility depends upon individual circumstances.

Medicare Rights Center (MRC)
1460 Broadway
New York, NY 10036-7393
Phone: 800-333-4114
Web site: www.medicarerights.org

MRC is a nonprofit organization dedicated to ensuring the rights of seniors and people with disabilities to quality, affordable health care. Several pamphlets are available for nominal fees.

National Committee to Preserve Social Security & Medicare (NCPSSM)
10 G Street, NE, Suite 600
Washington, DC 20002
Phone: 800-966-1935
Web site: www.ncpssm.org

The National Committee, an advocacy and education organization, is dedicated to protecting and enhancing federal programs vital to seniors' health and economic well-being. It has published the free brochure "Entitlements: What You Need to Know" plus consumer materials on many other subjects. Write or go online for a list of publications.

Paralyzed Veterans of America (PVA)
Veterans Benefits Department
801 18th Street, NW
Washington, DC 20006
Phone: 800-424-8200
Web site: www.pva.org

PVA is a veterans' service organization chartered by Congress to provide benefits, counseling, and claims representation for all veterans. These services are free of charge.

United Seniors Health Council (USHC)
409 3rd Street, SW, Suite 200
Washington, DC 20024
Phone: 202-479-6673
Web site: www.unitedseniorshealth.org

USHC annually publishes a special report, "Medicare Health Plan Choices: Consumer Update." Send a check for $4 (includes shipping and handling).

Part III

Private Long-Term Care Insurance

The fastest-growing segment of our society is the population 85 years and older. Since this population is at greatest risk of needing long-term care, it is not surprising that the number of people in nursing homes and needing help at home is expected to increase greatly.

Nursing home care is expensive. In 2000, MetLife Mature Market Institute reported the national average cost of a private room in a nursing home was roughly $55,000 a year. In some parts of the country and at particular nursing homes, the cost is significantly higher. Home care can cost $15 to $50 per hour. Realizing that the cost of long-term care exceeds their financial resources, many people are concerned about how they will pay for it. In order to meet this concern, insurance companies offer long-term care insurance for services received at home, in a nursing home, in an assisted living facility, or in an adult day service center.

Part III discusses the pros and cons of long-term care insurance, helps you decide if you need insurance, and explains the basics for selecting the best policy for you. Previous chapters explored various ways other than private insurance to pay for long-term care. You are strongly encouraged to read these earlier chapters before you consider long-term care insurance.

This guide does not tell you that you should or should not buy long-term care insurance. That decision is yours. It does explain how to assess your need for insurance and how to evaluate a policy. In Appendix A, you will find a worksheet to help you compare policies.

Long-term care insurance is an important type of coverage that protects you from catastrophic long-term care expenses. The policy pays a set amount of money for each day you are confined in a facility or receive care in the community, or the policy might reimburse you up to the maximum amount for the care received. Most companies provide flexibility in choosing benefit options to best meet individual needs.

You may learn about a policy from an insurance agent or from information sent to you in the mail by an association or employer. Some employers offer a group policy to employees, retirees, and family members. An association that sponsors a long-term care policy to members usually offers the same policy the company sells directly to individuals. Not all group policies have better benefits or are less expensive than individual policies. Do not assume that an employer's group policy or one sponsored by an association is better or cheaper than an individual policy you buy directly from an agent. It is very important that you compare policies yourself.

Who Pays for Nursing Home Care?

- *Medicare does not pay for long-term nursing home care.* Medicare covers a limited number of days for skilled care in a Medicare-approved facility. The average length of stay covered by Medicare is 28 days. Medicare pays 100 percent of costs for the first 20 days.

- *Medicaid pays for long-term nursing home care.* Medicaid pays for almost half of the nation's nursing home care costs. To be eligible for Medicaid, you must meet income and asset limits. Approximately 10 percent of Medicaid patients enter a nursing home as private-pay patients, spend down their assets, and become eligible for Medicaid.

- *One-third of nursing home costs are paid by individuals.* About 33 percent of the country's nursing home care cost is paid out-of-pocket by individuals. Currently, long-term care insurance pays about 5 percent. This is expected to increase as more insurance policies are sold.

Long-term care insurance is different from health insurance and life insurance. Health insurance pays for medical care; it does not pay for personal or custodial care. Life insurance protects your family in case of your death. Lately, some life insurance policies offer the option to use a portion of the death benefit for medical or long-term care. If you no longer need to protect your family, then using the life insurance benefit to help pay for needed care makes sense. However, if you are buying protection in case you need long-term care, a long-term care insurance policy will generally provide better coverage than an optional rider attached to a life insurance policy.

In general, long-term care policies are reimbursement plans. The policy pays a percentage (up to 100 percent) of actual charges up to a chosen maximum amount for care received. A policy that pays $100 per day may seem reasonable today if a nursing home costs $120 per day in your community. However, nursing home costs, like other health and medical costs, are rising much more rapidly than the general inflation rate. Ten years from now, $100 a day may pay for only a small portion of the cost of your care. In response to this need, many insurance companies offer an assortment of inflation-adjustment options on their long-term care policies.

Two basic types of policies are sold today—classic and integrated policies. The classic policy is an older product and usually covers nursing home and assisted living facility care, with an option of attaching a rider for home and community-based care. With the newer integrated policy, you purchase what is called a "pool of funds" that, after you meet the policy's eligibility requirements, you may use as you determine for a continuum of long-term care needs including home care, adult day health care, assisted living, and nursing home services. The pool of funds is calculated by multiplying the amount of the daily benefit you select times the number of days in the benefit period you choose. So if your daily benefit rate is $150 and the benefit period is 3 years (1,095 days), your pool of funds to draw upon would total $163,500.

Depending on your circumstances, either the classic or the integrated policy may be more suitable for you. Because medical requirements for coverage for the two types of policies can vary, you may have a better chance of being accepted under one type of policy than the other type.

The premium for a policy depends on several factors, such as:

- *Your age when you buy the policy.* In general, the younger you are when you buy, the lower your premiums.

- *Deductible or elimination period.* Most policies begin paying after you have been confined to a facility or declared to be qualified by virtue of meeting other criteria for a certain number of days, called the deductible or elimination period. Usually, the longer the deductible period, the lower the premium.
- *Benefits paid.* This includes the daily benefit amount and the length of the benefit period. The more money the policy pays or the longer time the policy covers services, the higher the premium.

Virtually all companies offer a level premium. This does not mean that the premium will remain the same. It means that you will continue to pay the premium charged to someone at the age you were when you originally bought the policy. The company, with approval from the state insurance department, may raise premiums for all policyholders within the state. The company cannot single out you or anyone else for an increase due to attained age or health condition. However, there is a possibility that premiums may increase. A company or association may have priced the policy too low in the beginning or may have experienced more

Long-Term Care Insurance Policy Annual Costs

All premiums below assume a $100 per day benefit with 5 percent compounded inflation protection. The ranges vary from a 90- to 100-day elimination period, from 2 years to an unlimited benefit length, and from a policy with a marital discount to one without. The $100 per day is for illustrative purposes only.

Age	Basic Coverage, Facility Only Premium range	Comprehensive Coverage, Facility and Community-Based Care Premium range
55	$375 to $1,100	$550 to $1,800
65	$700 to $2,000	$1,000 to $3,000
75	$1,560 to $4,700	$2,250 to $7,000

Source: N. P. Morith, Inc., Princeton, New Jersey, www.npmorith.com

claims than expected. The company could choose to offset any realized losses by raising premiums.

Long-term care policies vary widely. They differ in the benefits they offer, conditions in the contract, and the premiums. Evaluate policies carefully to see which one has benefits that fit your needs at a premium that fits your budget. The chart on the previous page indicates how premiums can vary for different policy levels purchased at different ages.

7

Insurance to Pay for Long-Term Care

There are a number of things to consider in buying long-term care insurance:

- Long-term care is expensive and can easily drain your financial resources. This prospect is frightening to many of us. Special insurance is available to help pay for this catastrophic expense. However, the insurance may also be expensive and can be of limited value if it is not properly designed. Therefore, while insurance is available, not every policy is the same, and it may not be the best solution for everyone.

- Furthermore, long-term care insurance is still a relatively new product. The policies have changed substantially since this type of insurance first came on the market and will continue to change as more information about long-term care utilization is learned. Indeed, federal law affects some changes in policies issued after January 1, 1997, if these policies are to be considered qualified for tax purposes. The law clearly allows you to treat at least a portion of long-term care insurance premiums on tax-qualified policies as medical expenses.

- Even if long-term care insurance is right for you, you should be careful how much insurance you buy. If you buy a high-cost policy that you can afford today, you may not be able to afford the premiums years from now.

■ Finally, whatever the recent or future changes, as a responsible consumer, you need to understand the basics of long-term care insurance policies and to purchase a policy most appropriate for you.

This chapter first discusses if long-term care insurance is right for you. The focus then shifts to an explanation of the tax implications of long-term care insurance. The chapter next focuses on the factors affecting the cost of insurance and provides a worksheet to assist you in determining how much insurance you should buy. This is followed by a discussion on what to look for and what to avoid in a policy and the pros and cons of options you can include in your policy. The chapter concludes by providing consumer tips for buying long-term care insurance.

Should You Buy Long-Term Care Insurance?

Your personal philosophy about participating in financial planning, leaving an inheritance, and taking risks plays an important role in deciding whether to purchase long-term care insurance. Buying insurance may make you feel secure, knowing you are protected. On the other hand, you may feel it is an unnecessary expense for a policy you may never need.

Long-term care insurance is available for people who are concerned about financing their possible future need for long-term care, either in an institutional setting or in their home, without depleting most of their assets. If your health is such that you expect to enter a nursing home or need home health care services in the next year or two, you will probably not find a policy to cover the admission except at exorbitant rates. Therefore, you need to buy this insurance before the need for long-term care is evident. Many companies will not sell to people in their eighties without severely restricting the amount of insurance you can buy.

You have your own unique family arrangement, financial situation, and medical history. All these factors influence whether you should buy long-term care insurance, and if you do, which policy.

Facts You Should Know

In making a decision whether or not to buy long-term care insurance, you need to understand your risk for needing nursing home or home health care services. Calculation of this risk is complicated, and results depend on the study and methodology used. Much more information is available about the probability of needing nursing home care than home health care services.

Your Chances of Needing Nursing Home Care. According to a 1997 research article in *Medical Care*, at age 65, you have a 43 percent likelihood of being in a nursing home at least once during your lifetime. However, since half of nursing home stays are short, usually 3 months or less, you have only a 23 percent likelihood of staying in a nursing home for more than 1 year; and a 9 percent likelihood of staying more than 5 years. Remember, it is the long stay in the nursing home with the associated catastrophic expense from which you are protecting yourself. Individual probability depends upon factors such as personal or family medical history and the availability of caregiver support from a spouse or other family members. Because women are more likely to be widowed and because their average life span is longer than that for men, they are more likely to need a long stay in a nursing home.

Average Length of Stay in a Nursing Home. According to the 1997 National Nursing Home Survey's discharge findings, the average stay in a nursing home for persons 65 and over was 290 days. Over 66 percent of these nursing home discharges stayed 3 months or less, 8 percent stayed 3 to 6 months, and 7 percent stayed 6 to 12 months. Only 10 percent of these nursing home residents' length of stay was from 1 to 3 years.

Of the people who stayed in a nursing home for 3 months or less, 74 percent had a prior hospitalization. These short-stay patients typically die quickly or are discharged home. A typical short-stay patient first develops an acute medical condition while residing in the community, is hospital-

---

What Are Your Chances of a Long Stay in a Nursing Home?

Length of stay in a nursing home	Chances for men	Chances for women
Enter sometime in your life	33%	52%
3 months or more	22%	41%
1 year or more	14%	31%
More than 5 years	4%	13%

Source: Medical Care, 1997.

ized, receives skilled care in a nursing home, and returns to the community. Medicare usually pays for some of this care.

Long-stay patients are more likely (43 percent) to be admitted directly from the community as the result of chronic degenerative conditions. Long-stay patients generally require custodial care upon entering the nursing home and stay for an average of 2 years.

Long-term care insurance should help pay for a possible long stay in a nursing home when you come directly from the community and primarily need custodial care.

Cost of a Nursing Home Stay. The national average cost for a private room for private-pay patients was roughly $55,000 per year ($153 per day) in 2000. Depending on the geographic area as well as the particular nursing home, this cost can vary between $40,000 and $80,000 per year. Medical and nursing home costs have been increasing annually far faster than the consumer price index. At a modest inflation rate of 6 percent, the average nursing home will cost almost $200 per day in 2005, and over $260 per day in 2010. The accompanying chart shows the effect of inflation on nursing home costs.

In addition, residents may have to finance costs associated with maintaining their personal residences if they anticipate returning to it or have other family members who intend to live there.

Effect of Inflation on Daily Rates for Nursing Home Care

Inflation rate	2000	2005	2010
5%	$140	$179	$229
6%	$147	$197	$264
7%	$154	$215	$303
8%	$162	$237	$349

Your Chances of Needing Home Care. Estimates of the likelihood of needing home care and how much home care may be needed are much less precise than those for nursing home care. A 1989 study by the Brookings Institution indicates that 28 percent of people age 65 will use no formal or paid home care visits in their lifetime, while almost 30 percent will use from 1 to 60 visits. One-quarter of the 65-year-olds will receive between 61 and 365 home care visits in their lifetime. Approximately 17 percent will have more than 365 visits.

Factors That Influence Your Decision

When determining whether you should buy long-term care insurance, carefully review your entire situation. Factors to consider are your health and your financial resources.

Your Health.   Your current age and health status and the medical history of your family are among the critical factors that influence your probability of entering a nursing home or needing home health care. Chronic health conditions, such as diabetes, respiratory ailments, and Alzheimer's disease, may lead to deteriorating health and increasing dependence on long-term care. Much of your health is inherited. If your parents lived to their nineties, chances are you will also. Your lifestyle also has a major influence. If you smoked most of your life, you will most likely have a shorter life span than if you did not. If you watch what you eat, exercise regularly, cease smoking, and stay healthy, chances are you will live longer.

Financial Resources.   The decision to purchase long-term care insurance largely hinges on two separate but related financial questions. First, can you afford long-term care insurance premiums over the long run? Second, do your assets amount to enough to warrant protecting them with long-term care insurance, but not enough to cover the full cost of long-term care? In other words, does this insurance make economic sense for someone in your financial situation? The question of affordability of long-term care insurance is comparatively easy for you to analyze since you know your budget. Premiums can be expensive and in all likelihood will increase over time. You have to assess your current budget and insofar as possible estimate your future financial situation, particularly if you have a limited, fixed retirement income. Although this income may seem adequate early in your retirement, you may later feel strapped due to inflation. If you stop paying premiums and let a policy lapse in the future because it becomes too burdensome, you stand to lose your investment of premiums, unless you have a nonforfeiture benefit, discussed later in this chapter.

It is difficult to give you any precise guideline about how much income and assets you should have before you take on the burden of paying insurance premiums. Your common sense can be your best guide. For example, you should not buy this insurance if you must pay the premiums from your savings or if you have to make significant lifestyle changes in order to pay premiums. Generally speaking, each member of your household should have at least $25,000 to $35,000 in annual retirement income depending on where you reside and $75,000 in assets, excluding your home and car, before thinking of buying long-term care insurance. Each person's or family's situation is unique, and so the suggested income and asset minimums should not be treated as absolute.

The second question of whether long-term care insurance makes economic sense or is appropriate for you is a far more complicated issue. It boils down to determining what amount of assets you should have in order to make it worthwhile to protect them with insurance. Of course, it is natural to want to protect your assets, no matter what they are. However, if you have few assets, you may not need insurance because Medicaid can help absorb nursing home costs. Conversely, if you are wealthy, you have the option of self-funding your potential nursing home costs, or you can easily afford to buy insurance. It is middle-class individuals who have the tough decision to make about the economic sense of insurance.

Because there are so many variables and because individuals' situations differ so much, no convenient, accurate formula applicable to everyone exists for calculating at what point long-term care insurance makes economic sense for you. The answer in part comes down to how many of your assets you would have to spend before you would become eligible for Medicaid and how willing you are to spend these assets.

Protecting Assets for Spouse or Children

Many people are concerned about depleting their hard-earned assets to pay for long-term care instead of bequeathing them to their spouse and children. Long-term care insurance protects assets, thus leaving more in your estate at death to be passed on to a loved one or a favorite institution.

If you are married, you should seriously evaluate what your financial position would be if one spouse might need long-term care. A lengthy, expensive stay in a nursing home could easily wipe out the majority of your assets, leaving the spouse remaining in the community without the financial resources to live the active life that was planned. However, even without an insurance policy, some assets are protected by Medicaid for a nursing home resident's spouse who remains living in the community.

If your spouse enters a nursing home and is expected to remain there, Medicaid takes a snapshot of your finances. Protected assets are the primary residence, car, personal belongings, liquid assets (such as saving accounts, mutual funds, stocks, bonds, and certificates of deposit) up to the Medicaid asset limit, life insurance with a face value under $1,500, and a burial fund of less than $1,500 for each spouse. The remaining assets are available to pay for expenses of the spouse in the nursing home and must be spent before Medicaid will pay the nursing home costs. Refer to Chapter 6 for a review of Medicaid.

Protecting assets for your children is another question. First, consider whether you really need to leave an inheritance for your children, and if you do, how much. Many children, when asked, do not expect to be left a sizable estate. If you decide you would like to leave some assets to your children or to others and also benefit from Medicaid support, sheltering your assets by setting up a trust fund now requires implementation before you may need Medicaid assistance, at least 5 years in advance. Refer to Chapter 6 for a brief discussion of the Medicaid-related issues about trusts and the transfer of assets.

You can also transfer a limited amount of assets tax-free to your children or others by given them a gift of property or money. Under current tax law, you can give up to $10,000 per person per year without paying a gift tax. In order to protect a transfer of assets under Medicaid, the transfer must be for fair market value or be completed more than 36 months before you apply for Medicaid.

Family Situation

The availability of family members or friends to provide some needed care is an important consideration. The presence of a primary caregiver, such as a spouse or other close family member, often delays the need for nursing home care. A long-term care insurance policy, especially a policy with substantial home care benefits, can relieve the caregiver, thus extending the time you can stay at home and avoid entering a nursing home.

You may not have a primary caregiver. Your spouse may have died, and your children may live far away and not be able to provide needed care. If you do not have a primary caregiver, you will have to pay for long-term care assistance. Home care should cost less than nursing home care when it is used to supplement care from a caregiver. However, extensive 24-hour-a-day home care can cost as much as or more than a nursing home. People without a primary caregiver are more likely to enter a nursing home sooner and stay longer.

Special Considerations for Women

Three factors suggest that women may have somewhat different needs for long-term care insurance than men. First, because they have a longer average life span, and if married, tend to outlive their husbands, women have a higher risk of needing institutional care at some point in their lives. Second, older women, whether they are single or widowed, tend to have lower incomes and fewer financial resources than men. Third, as they grow older, they are also more likely than men to live alone and not have a spouse or other family member available as the primary provider of home care.

When weighing long-term care insurance in light of these risk factors, women may need to focus more on the benefits of institutional care rather than home care because home care benefits may not provide enough hours of care to overcome the need for nursing home care for a person living alone. Therefore, policies covering just the facility merit women's special attention. Further, when a wife purchases long-term care insurance, she may also need to take into account whether she can pay the premium if her spouse dies first and her income is reduced.

Your Attitude about Medicaid

Medicaid is available to pay for medical care, nursing home care, and some home care for anyone who cannot pay for it. The program is a joint federal-state welfare program that may be subject to future changes and restrictions. How you feel about receiving Medicaid assistance may influence your decision to buy insurance.

You may want to avoid Medicaid at all costs, or you may feel that you paid taxes throughout your lifetime and deserve to benefit from this tax-supported program. Medicaid pays for just over half of the nursing home expenses in the nation. Many people being supported by Medicaid in nursing homes entered too poor to pay themselves. Approximately 15 to 25 percent of nursing home residents spend down their assets to become eligible for Medicaid.

People on Medicaid at the time of admission have fewer choices of nursing homes than private-pay patients do. Because Medicaid pays less than private patients pay for care, some nursing homes do not or prefer not to accept Medicaid patients. However, people with income and assets that will pay for about a year of nursing home care usually have their choice of homes.

Nursing homes are not supposed to discriminate against people who start as private-pay patients and then go on Medicaid when their money runs out. A facility cannot discharge you or treat you differently just because Medicaid is paying. However, sometimes nursing homes do make changes. A nursing home administrator might say that a Medicaid bed is not available, or may try to discharge a Medicaid patient for some other reason. Enforcement of nursing home regulations varies among states. The nursing home ombudsman program, available through your local area agency on aging, monitors this potential problem.

Risks Involved

How much of a risk taker or risk averter you are influences your decision to buy insurance. A risk averter would buy the insurance to be safe. A risk taker may decide to gamble. If you do not buy insurance, you run the risk of needing long-term care and having to spend your assets to pay for it. If you do buy insurance, you run the risk that you will die without needing long-term care.

The nature of insurance is the pooling of risks. Some people who buy the insurance may never need long-term care; others may receive the full benefit from the policy. Pooling spreads the risks and reduces the premiums for everyone. There is no crystal ball for you to see the future. You have to make the decision based on what you think is likely to happen.

Ability to Self-Fund

Unless you are wealthy or are able to save the equivalent or more of your long-term care insurance premium over a span of many years, the idea of self-funding or self-insuring your potential long-term care needs ordinarily is not a viable option. Self-funding means saving your own money or investing it for later use to pay for your nursing home or home health care.

The problem with self-insuring is that you do not know when you will need the protection. To acquire an adequate nest egg equal to the total benefits of an insurance policy, you will have to save $1,500 to $3,000 for each of 20 to 25 years and get a very good rate of return on your investment. If you are one of the few people able to do this, you may have enough to provide at least as good protection as if you had bought a long-term care policy. However, if you do not buy insurance and a few years later you unexpectedly need nursing home care, your savings will not pay as much as the insurance would have.

Some people already have savings or liquid assets sufficient to pay for 2 or 3 years of nursing home care without insurance or Medicaid assistance. For such persons the issue is whether or not they are prepared to use these assets for any needed long-term care or to preserve them for an inheritance by purchasing insurance.

Self-funding is not the same as insurance. It does not provide the short-term protection that an insurance policy does. Buying insurance protects you from the possible risk of paying for nursing home care before you accumulate adequate resources.

Future of Public Policy for Long-Term Care

Another factor to consider when planning a number of years ahead is that the country's health care system is in a state of flux. The present and projected costs of long-term care have become a great concern to federal and state policymakers. They continue to consider ways to control and limit the cost to the government for long-term care. Medicaid regulations and finances are a special focus of possible reform. If you are attempting to protect yourself against health care costs some 10 or 20 years in the future, it is almost impossible to anticipate what public policy will be or what public funds will be available to pay these costs.

Keeping Your Decision in Proper Perspective

Check your Medicare, health, and supplemental insurance policies to understand what coverage you already have and what you feel you still need. Be careful not to become so concerned with insuring yourself against the possibility of problems arising in the future that you allow insufficient time or money to enjoy your life today.

Keep a good balance so that you enjoy all stages of your life in relative comfort. Beware of those who would sell their products and services by stirring up fear and anxiety. With your life experience, have the confidence to use your own good judgment to evaluate what you hear.

Tax Treatment of Long-Term Care Insurance

In 1996 Congress passed the Health Insurance Portability and Accountability Act (HIPAA) that established the tax treatment of long-term care insurance. Policies issued after January 1, 1997, with tax benefits are classified as tax-qualified policies, and those without any tax benefit are classified as non-tax-qualified policies. Also, some policies issued before 1997 are considered tax-qualified policies. The difference between tax-qualified policies and non-tax-qualified policies available to insurable consumers has led to some confusion about which policy is the best option to consider. The advantages and disadvantages of each are described below.

Tax-Qualified Policies

The most important advantage is the tax treatment of the benefits and premiums. Benefits received by insured policyholders to reimburse them for approved services are tax-free; policies paying the total purchased benefit outright have limits ($210 per day in 2002) on the amount that can be excluded from income. Premiums may be deductible as medical expenses, but before any deduction for premiums paid by an individual can be taken, an individual's total allowable medical expenses must exceed 7½ percent of his or her adjusted gross income. There are maximum deduction limits based upon age (see the accompanying chart). Note that employer contributions toward premiums are excluded from the employee's taxable income.

These policies must meet stringent consumer protection standards, and companies selling these policies must follow certain administrative and marketing procedures or face significant fines.

Benefit triggers, which activate the payment of

Tax-Deductible Limits (2002) for Long-Term Care Insurance Premiums

Your age	Maximum premium allowed for deduction
40 years or under	$240
41–50	$450
51–60	$900
61–70	$2,390
71 and older	$2,990

Note: These dollar limits are indexed according to increases in the medical care component of the consumer price index. *Source:* N. P. Morith, Inc., Princeton, NJ, www.npmorith.com

benefits, may be more restrictive than those for non-tax-qualified policies. Disability must be expected to last at least 90 days. You must be unable to do two of the following activities of daily living (ADLs):

bathing, dressing, toileting, eating, staying continent, or transferring without substantial assistance. "Medical necessity" is not allowed as a trigger. For cognitive impairment to be covered, a person must require "substantial supervision," and the impairment must be severe.

Non-Tax-Qualified Policies

Benefit triggers (which activate the payment of benefits) may be more lenient than those for tax-qualified policies. There is no requirement for a 90-day certification of anticipated need for help with two or more activities of daily living. Policies can offer a different combination of benefit triggers. "Medical necessity" and/or other measures of disability can be offered as benefit triggers. Policies don't have to require "substantial supervision" to trigger benefits for cognitive impairment.

The Department of the Treasury has still to rule on the tax treatment of benefits received from non-tax-qualified policies. Income from those benefits is not specifically exempt from federal taxation (as it is for tax-qualified policies). Due to the lack of clarity, there is a gray area in enforcement of any taxation of these benefits. Until the regulations are issued or there is a federal tax case to decide the law, there could be variations in tax treatment in an audit. Moreover, you cannot deduct any part of your annual premium if itemizing tax deductions. IRS 1099 LTC forms, now issued by insurance companies, indicate whether or not the policy is tax-qualified.

These policies may not necessarily have the more stringent consumer protection standards required of tax-qualified policies.

Which Policy Is Right for Me?

If you decide that buying insurance is the right decision for you, or you just want to evaluate some long-term care policies, you need to keep in mind the two basic types of policies available today—classic and integrated, briefly discussed earlier in the Part III opening section—and to understand the benefits package in a policy. The classic policy basically covers nursing home care. A rider for home care also can be added. Some newer policies make provision for "alternate forms of care" such as assisted living. With integrated policies, which are a newer product and generally more expensive than classic policies, your benefit is a fixed pool of funds that you can draw upon to meet a range of long-term care expenses from home care to nursing homes.

Some insurance companies sell one package of benefits, while others offer a variety of options for you to select. As more and more companies are offering a variety of policies, do not settle for a policy unless you are sure it meets your needs. Companies that offer options in coverage allow you to tailor a policy to meet your needs. The premium of a policy depends on the coverage you choose. If you select the high option for every choice offered, you may find yourself overinsured, or, at the very least, with a very expensive policy.

All policies have exclusions, restrictions, and limitations. By understanding the terms of coverage for the policy, you are more likely to buy the best policy for your needs. This section discusses how much insurance you need; presents advantages and disadvantages of various options; and discusses how exclusions, restrictions, and limitations affect your coverage.

How Much Insurance to Buy

The more insurance you buy, the more you will pay in premiums. The cost of insurance is based on three factors:

- *The daily benefit amount.* This is the amount the policy will pay for each day of covered services.
- *The benefit period.* This period is the length of time the policy will pay benefits, or the maximum value of benefits to be paid.
- *The deductible or elimination period.* This is the number of days you pay for services from your own funds before the policy starts to pay.

These three factors determine how much the insurance will cost for a person your age.

Most people live on a relatively fixed income during retirement. Social Security benefits and some pension plans have cost-of-living adjustments (COLAs), but much of your retirement income may not keep up with inflation. Although some expenses—such as clothing and maybe housing, if you have paid off your mortgage—decrease in retirement, other expenses, such as medical care and travel, may increase.

Virtually all companies offer a level premium. This does not mean that the premium is guaranteed to remain the same over time. It means that you will continue to pay the premium charged to someone at the age you were when you originally bought the policy. If you buy insurance at age

68, when you are 82, you will pay a premium the equivalent to whatever the company then charges for a new 68-year-old policyholder. With approval from the state insurance department, the company may raise premiums for all policyholders within the state. The company cannot single out you or anyone else for an increase due to attained age or a health condition. However, premiums can increase. Because a company may have priced the policy too low or may have experienced more claims than expected, it may attempt to offset any realized loss by requesting state approval to raise premiums. Since rates do increase, any insurance you buy should be affordable today as well as in the future.

Before you talk to an agent about buying insurance, evaluate your finances and decide how much you want to buy. Remember, the more you buy, the more the premiums will be. In case premiums increase, you should buy the amount of insurance that makes the policy easily affordable today and in the future.

Daily Benefit Amount. The daily benefit amount is the amount of money the company will pay for each covered day of service. Policies offer benefit amounts from $50 to $250 per day. How much you buy should depend on how much a nursing home costs in your community, how much you can pay for your long-term care from income, and how much insurance you can afford to buy. *There is no magic amount.*

Financial advisers usually suggest that you buy between two-thirds and three-quarters of the current daily cost of nursing homes in your community. The amount of the daily benefit you select depends on your personal circumstances and preferences. If you want to go to a more expensive nursing home, you may opt for a higher benefit amount. Or you can decide on a smaller benefit if you will have enough income to pay for some care. Basically, you are trying to save most of your assets by using available income and the insurance policy to pay for needed care.

Today's cost of nursing home care will increase in the years to come. To help your benefit amount keep up with inflation, you can buy a policy that adjusts the benefit amount. There are two basic types of adjustments: (1) an automatic annual inflation adjustment and (2) an option to buy additional benefit amounts periodically. Which is best for you depends on your situation.

The automatic annual inflation adjustment is usually 5 percent per year. Previously most policies offered only a simple rate of inflation. On a $100-a-day policy, a 5 percent adjustment will pay $150 per day in 10 years, or a $5 (5 percent of $100) increase every year. Today for a higher premium many policies offer a compound rate of inflation. In the same 10 years, a policy with a 5 percent compounded adjustment will pay $163 per day. The longer the adjustment, the bigger the difference between simple and compound rates of inflation. Policies also vary in the percentage offered.

Some policies offer the adjustment for 20 years, while other policies offer it until you reach a specific age, such as 86 years. Depending on your age when you buy the policy, one option may be better than the other. If you are 65, there is no difference. If you are over 65, then adjustment for 20 years is better; whereas if you are under 65, adjustment until you are 86 is better. The best protection is inflation adjustment until you die. Another type of inflation adjustment is the option to buy additional benefit amounts periodically. A policy may offer an adjustment based on the difference in the consumer price index every 3 years. This option gives you control over the benefit amount, but you may forget to increase the benefit when offered. You are also buying the added benefit amount at a higher premium level based on your attained age. Analysis of the two adjustments shows that for people under age 50 and for the first 10 years for older people, the option to buy may be less costly. However, if you do not expect to need long-term care until more than 10 years from now, the automatic adjustment is probably less costly.

Daily Benefit Amount Increased at Simple and Compound Rates (5%)

Year	Simple	Compound	Difference
0	$100	$100	$0
10	$150	$163	$13
15	$175	$208	$33
20	$200	$265	$65
25	$225	$339	$114
30	$250	$432	$182

Benefit Period. The benefit period is the length of time the policy will pay you the daily benefit for covered services. Lengths can vary from 1 year to a lifetime. Benefit periods usually are measured in number of days or maximum dollar amount. Each day you receive benefit from the policy counts against your policy maximum. If you received 3 months (90 days) of benefits from a 2-year (730 days) policy, you would have 640 days left to use later. Other policies measure the maximum in dollars. Simply multiply the daily benefit amount times the maximum number of days. A 2-year, $80-per-day policy will pay a maximum of $58,400. The money received from the policy counts against the dollar maximum. A lifetime policy does not have a maximum.

The benefit period that you need depends on the amount of assets you want to protect. Projecting into the future is difficult. You do not know when you will need long-term care, how much it will cost, how much you can pay from income, and how much you will have in assets. Instead of trying to guess future inflation rates, calculate how much you need using today's figures. Use the worksheet on pages 97 and 98 to calculate the benefit length that best meets your needs.

You may be tempted to buy an unlimited benefit period because you simply do not know how long you will need long-term care. Remember, the average long stay in a nursing home is just over 2 years. Instead, first select an optimal benefit amount; then select a benefit period that you can afford today and in the future.

Deductible (Elimination) Period.   Most policies require that you pay for needed care for a specified number of days, called the deductible or elimination period, before the policy starts to pay the daily benefit. Although a few policies offer a zero-day deductible period, they are more expensive and may require a tighter review of eligibility for benefits. The deductible period deters people from going into a nursing home unnecessarily.

Long-term care insurance is intended to help you in case you need a long stay in a nursing home. It is not intended to pay for medical care that may be paid by Medicare and your health insurance. A long-term care policy with a deductible period will not pay for a short stay, which usually is the result of a medical episode. Refer to Chapter 6 to learn how Medicare and your health insurance might pay for some, if not all, of this care. Even if the stay is expected to be long, you only have to pay for a short time before the policy starts paying the daily benefit.

Consider the affordability of the policy when deciding the best deductible period for you. Also, compare the difference in the cost of a shorter deductible period with the amount of money you would save by having the policy start paying sooner. Depending on your financial situation, select a deductible period that best meets your needs. Many people buy a policy with a deductible period between 20 and 100 days. It is important to recognize that you self-insure for the deductible period. For example, if you choose the

Calculate Your Optimum Benefit Period

1. *Daily cost of nursing home care:*
   Check in your community for the daily cost of a nursing home you might consider using. You can average the cost for different levels of care and from different nursing homes to arrive at a reasonable daily cost.

   Sample: $120 per day

   Average daily cost in your locality: _____

2. *Daily amount that can be paid from your income:*
   Decide how much you will be able to pay from your income. If you are a couple, figure that almost all your income will be needed to maintain one spouse in the community, leaving nothing to help pay for long-term care. If you plan to return to your home, some income is needed to maintain your house.

   Sample: John and Mary have a monthly income of $2,400. If one of them needs to go to a nursing home, they need $1,950 to pay monthly expenses, leaving $450 per month, or $15 per day, available to help pay for nursing home expenses.

   Sample: $15 per day

   Daily amount you can pay: _____

3. *Daily amount needed from assets:*
   Subtract the amount you can pay out of your income from the daily cost of long-term care. This gives you the amount you will pay from your assets or with an insurance policy. If you buy a policy that will pay the entire balance, the benefit period you should buy is the length of time you think you may need long-term care. Remember, only a small percentage of people stay in a nursing home for more than a year, and even fewer stay for more than 5 years. If you are afraid you might eventually get Alzheimer's disease or some other slowly deteriorating medical condition, you might consider a longer benefit period or even a lifetime benefit.

   continued

Sample: John and Mary need $105 per day for nursing home costs. They bought a policy that pays $80 per day, leaving $25 per day that they must pay from their assets.

Sample:		Your calculation
$120	per day cost	$ _____
−15	per day from income	− _____
$105	per day needed	$ _____
−80	policy benefit amount	− _____
$25	per day from assets	$ _____

4. *Number of days you need for a benefit period:*
   If some of your assets are needed to pay for your care, determine how long your assets will last before you will need to go on Medicaid. Remember, a policy that overlaps with Medicaid benefits the Medicaid program, not you. Divide the daily amount needed from assets into the total assets you have available to pay for your long-term care. Do not include your house, car, and personal belongings. If you are a couple, do not include the amount of assets Medicaid allows a spouse remaining in the community to protect, the so-called Medicaid spousal impoverishment limit (see Chapter 6). The result of the division is the number of days your assets will last. Round down to the nearest benefit level. If your assets would last for 900 days, a 2-year policy paying 730 days would be adequate. Be careful not to buy too much. Remember (1) your chance of an extremely long stay in a nursing home is small, and (2) the policy you buy must be affordable.

Sample: John and Mary have $40,000 in assets over the Medicaid spousal impoverishment limit that must be spent before Medicaid starts to pay. If they need to pay $25 per day from the assets to pay for needed care, their assets available to pay for nursing home care will last 1,600 days, or somewhat more than 4 years. So they should buy a policy with a benefit period of no more than 4 years.

100-day period and incur costs up to $100 a day, you would be self-insuring for $10,000. Policies differ on how they calculate a deductible period. A few policies require you to meet a new deductible period each time you need care. Most policies do not require consecutive days of care, but some require that you meet the new deductible if a specified period of time, usually 180 days, has elapsed between long-term care services. Many are now cumulative over the life of the policy.

Selecting a Policy

Nearly 120 companies sell long-term care insurance. The vast majority of policies currently being sold are individual policies. Group policies are also available through some associations as well as a growing number of employers, including the federal government, who offer this insurance as a benefit to employees and retirees. Group policies are not necessarily cheaper or better than individual policies.

You may receive information about a policy in the mail, or an insurance agent may contact you. As more companies continually change their policies, the decision of which policy to buy becomes harder. This section will help you to evaluate policies by discussing features to look for and to avoid in policies.

Underwriting Principles

Just because you want to buy long-term care insurance does not mean the company will necessarily sell you a policy. Insurance companies establish underwriting guidelines to determine if you are insurable. Most companies restrict the sale of a policy to people within a certain age range, usually between 40 and 79 years of age. Some companies offer policies to people as young as 18 years of age. A few companies will sell to people in their eighties and beyond, but with limitations. This may mean a possible limit to the benefit amount or benefit period.

Although companies differ in their underwriting guidelines, all companies need to collect enough premiums to cover expected expenditures for benefits paid. Companies may choose not to insure certain risks in order to limit expected costs and maintain affordable premiums.

To assess the risk associated with insuring you, companies require you to complete an application that asks questions about your health and may require permission to get copies of clinical notes from your doctor(s).

Based on your medical history, the company decides whether to insure you. Failure to disclose a medical condition or other pertinent information may result in cancellation of the policy or denial of payment later. This means that if after selling you a policy a company discovers you did not previously disclose a medical condition for which the company might deny you insurance, it may decide to deny your claim, cancel your policy, and maybe refund some of the premiums you paid.

It is in your best interest to answer all questions honestly and to disclose everything. However, it is a good idea to discuss this procedure with your doctor and to check your medical records to see if there is something that may need explaining. If the company denies you a policy, request an explanation for denial.

There could be a good possibility that there was a misunderstanding. You can then appeal the decision. If you are definitely denied coverage, you can apply to another company. Being denied coverage does not mean there is something wrong with you, or that you are going to die soon. It just means that the insurance company thinks that you are too great a risk for its particular type of business.

If you have real medical problems, be skeptical of a company that will sell you a policy. The company may not be making a wise business decision in selling insurance to a high-risk person. More importantly, the company may substantially raise premiums or may have little intention of paying your claim. A reputable, financially sound insurance company will not take high risks. If a policy is too good to be true, then something may very well be wrong.

Choosing a Company

A long-term care policy is only as good as the insurance company standing behind it. You can expect to pay premiums for many years before you submit any claims for long-term care. During this time, you are trusting that the company will pay the claim when it comes time for you to need long-term care. You are trusting that the company will have the financial resources and will honor the policy. This takes a great deal of trust. By the time you realize that there may be problems, it could be too late for you to do anything about it.

Selecting a company is a very critical consideration in buying a policy. Very few companies have much experience paying claims from long-term care policies. However, there are some ways you can screen the companies.

First, select a financially sound company. A.M. Best, Standard & Poor's, Duff & Phelps, Moody's, and Weiss Ratings publish safety ratings of insurance companies. Insurance policies are not rated. Updates to ratings are published monthly, quarterly, and annually. You can find the published financial rating of companies in the reference section of your library. However, even if a company has a high rating, this should not be the sole basis for selecting that company's policy. You also need to evaluate a policy based on its cost for the benefits provided to suit your needs.

Second is the reputation and claims-paying history of the company. A good financial rating may not be enough. Some highly rated companies have been known to deny or delay paying claims in health insurance. If the company adheres to this practice for health insurance claims, there is a good chance it will do so for long-term care insurance claims down the road. Call your state insurance department for information on the complaints about specific companies. If your insurance department does not collect this information, judge the company by your own sense of reputation. A well-known company is less likely to risk bad publicity for this type of activity.

The third consideration is the number of policies sold and the company's commitment to this market. If more claims or more expensive claims are experienced than expected, a company may request an increase in premiums. The smaller the number of policyholders, the heftier the increase may need to be. Although the number of companies selling long-term care insurance has grown steadily over the past 5 years, some companies have stopped selling policies or have even sold the policies in force to another insurance company. About 120 companies have sold nearly 6 million policies. A dozen companies have sold four-fifths of these policies. Do not take the company's word for commitment to this market. Ask how many policies have been sold and if the company has ever discontinued selling an insurance product.

Requirements for Coverage

A long-term care insurance policy will pay the daily benefit only after you meet the requirements for coverage as described in the policy. These requirements are meant to ensure that long-term care services are actually necessary. Obviously most people do not want to live in a nursing home but do so because they need to. However, insurance companies are wary of people being placed in a nursing home just because insurance will pay for it.

Policies differ on the extent of medical criteria required for benefits. Earlier policies required that a person stay at least 3 days in a hospital and be admitted to a nursing home within 30 days of hospital discharge. Almost half of short-stay patients are admitted from a hospital. However, long-term care insurance usually does not cover this type of stay. Most long-stay residents come directly from the community. Policies that require a prior hospital stay have less than a 40 percent probability of paying the benefit if you go into a nursing home for a long stay.

If you have one of these older policies, you may want to consider replacing it with a newer, better policy. Depending upon how long ago you bought your original policy, you may find that the newer policy will be more expensive because you are older. This is not, however, universally true since many companies are finding better than expected experience and are actually able to reduce rates on newer policies. It is important to obtain a full and accurate proposal prior to making any decisions on replacing or altering an existing policy. If you cannot afford a better policy, you may want to consider whether the policy you currently have is worth keeping. But it is important to check the company that sold the policy for upgrades or riders that may be less expensive than a new policy. You should also check with a number of companies about possibly supplementing the old policy with a new one at a lower daily benefit.

No policies sold today require a prior hospitalization. However, just because the policy does not require a prior hospital stay does not mean that it is a good policy.

Many, especially older, policies have other medical criteria, such as an illness, injury, sickness, or other medical necessity requirement, which must be met before benefits are paid. The older a person is, the greater the probability that long-term care is needed because of old age, and not necessarily because of a medical episode. Terms such as *illness*, *sickness*, *diagnosis*, or *injury* imply an acute onset of a medical condition. This raises the question of whether an underlying chronic medical condition, such as high blood pressure or arthritis, would qualify as an illness requiring admission to a nursing home. Policies with these terms are vague. A reputable company would most likely pay the claim if your physician certified that you needed long-term care. However, other companies may question the physician's certification and deny your claim because long-term care is not medically necessary by their definition if it is not clearly stated in the policy. Other terms found in policies that imply a medical reason for long-term care are *medical treatment plan, diagnosis, in accordance with medical practice,* or *nursing care.*

Read your policy carefully. If you already have a policy that requires your physician to certify that long-term care is medically necessary or is due to illness or injury, you may want to consider upgrading the policy. If you decide to keep the policy, be sure you see your physician enough times to thoroughly document your medical condition in your medical record.

A reasonable criterion to determine payment of benefits is whether you need long-term care due to one of two conditions: (1) physical impairment, defined as needing assistance with activities of daily living (ADLs) such as eating, dressing, bathing, transferring from bed to chair, and toileting; or (2) cognitive impairment, defined as diminished mental capacity from Alzheimer's disease or other dementia that requires supervision to protect self or others from harm. A third condition, due to illness or injury, may be added if it is clearly a third option and is not part of the other two conditions.

Many policies require that you need assistance in two or three activities of daily living to qualify for benefits. Assistance may be defined as total reliance on another person or supervisory assistance. A policy that requires total reliance is stricter than a policy that allows you just to need someone to watch in case you have problems. Be careful of the numbers game, referring to the number of ADLs needed to qualify for benefits. Bathing is usually the first ADL with which a person may need assistance. A policy requiring two ADLs that does not include bathing is no better than a policy requiring three ADLs that does include bathing.

The definitions in a policy of ADLs are a critical point to examine. There are no standard definitions nor a fixed set of ADLs included in every policy. Definitions of the same ADL vary from company to company. And, in fact, the same company's definition can vary from state to state since policies are regulated differently in each state. As an example, one policy's definition of bathing can include sponge bathing outside a bathtub, while another policy's definition might mean washing in a shower or bathtub. Subtle differences in definitions can mean the difference between coverage or not.

Another important condition for qualifying for benefits is cognitive ability. People with Alzheimer's disease or other dementia may be able to perform activities of daily living, but may not be aware of person, place, or time. Cognitive impairment is the deterioration in or loss of intellectual capacity. A person with cognitive impairment may exhibit abusive behavior, poor judgment, or bizarre habits. The statement in the policy that says it covers Alzheimer's disease is not good enough. A good long-term care policy will pay for needed supervision due to cognitive impairment, regardless of whether the person has impairments with any of the ADLs.

Activities of Daily Living

Basic Activities

Most Common

- *Bathing.* The ability to wash your body in a shower or bathtub, including getting in and out
- *Dressing.* The ability to put on and take off clothes that are worn daily

On Demand

- *Transferring.* The ability to move body weight, such as from bed to chair
- *Toileting.* The ability to get to the bathroom, to get on and off the commode, to perform needed functions, and to clean oneself afterward

On Schedule

- *Eating.* The ability to move food to your mouth after food has been prepared

Ancillary Activities

- *Continence.* The ability to voluntarily control bowel and bladder functions or to maintain personal hygiene with the aid of equipment
- *Medications.* The ability to maintain a schedule and to administer medications

Note: These definitions are general and may not match those in specific policies. The identification of particular activities of daily living and the actual definitions of these activities can vary from policy to policy.

Policies should not combine any of the three conditions for needing long-term care. A policy that bases needing assistance with ADLs on medical criteria such as illness, injury, or medical necessity is no better than a policy that requires medical criteria without the mention of ADLs. A policy that requires needing assistance with ADLs due to cognitive impairment will not help a person with Alzheimer's disease who often can easily perform these activities but still needs constant supervision.

Levels and Setting of Care

Long-term care policies should cover all levels of care: skilled, intermediate, and most important, custodial. As presented in Chapter 6, Medicare and your health insurance may pay for some skilled care in a nursing home or at home, but they do not pay for custodial care. Only long-term care insurance is available to pay for this level of care.

The policy should not require skilled care before paying for custodial care and should not require nursing home care before paying for home care. Look for a policy that pays for custodial care as long as you meet the eligibility requirement.

Medicare and your medigap insurance will pay for up to 100 days of skilled care in a nursing home after a hospitalization. If you remain in the nursing home after this period, you will pay. A long-term care policy should pay benefits for all levels of care in a nursing home. Medicare pays for skilled care at home for recuperation and rehabilitation as long as you continue to improve. Although you may need a long-term care policy to pay for some skilled care, you need a long-term care policy primarily to pay benefits for custodial or personal care. Home care benefits should include home care aides, adult day health services, and personal aides.

The primary settings of care are institutional care and at-home care. The distinction between these two settings is not as obvious as you might think. If you receive services in your home or apartment, it is obviously home care. If you are admitted to a licensed skilled nursing home, it is nursing home care. However, you may live in a retirement home or special facility for seniors. Most policies consider care received in these settings as home care. What you consider institutional care may be considered home care by the company.

Some states call custodial nursing homes domiciliary care or assisted care facilities. Policies should state coverage for facilities that provide only custodial care. Most policies define a nursing home as a facility that has at least one registered nurse, maintains medical records, and administers medications. In most states, licensed domiciliary care or assisted living facilities have these same requirements but should be covered by the language of new long-term care insurance policies. However, if the policy requires that the facility primarily provides nursing care, assisted living and domiciliary care facilities will not be covered.

Definitions of Levels of Care

- *Skilled nursing care* is the type of care performed by a registered nurse (RN) or other skilled medical worker such as a therapist. It is always provided under the supervision of a physician.
- *Intermediate nursing care* requires a doctor's orders and trained medical personnel. The main distinction is that the patient needs this care only occasionally, two or three times a week.
- *Custodial care* is not medical and does not require the services of skilled medical workers. Custodial care usually consists of assistance with activities of daily living such as eating, dressing, bathing, and walking. Custodial care is the most common nursing home care provided.

Settings of Care

- *Home care* consists of a wide variety of services delivered to you in your home. They can range from skilled services like those provided by nurses, social workers, and therapists to assistance given by health aides and even homemakers.
- An *adult day health services center* is a facility that provides socialization and some health care during the day.
- *Respite care* is temporary care, usually overnight, in a facility or at home.
- An *assisted living facility* is a facility that provides personal care, assistance with ADLs, and supervision to persons who do not need nursing care.
- A *nursing home* is usually defined as a specially qualified facility that has staff and equipment to provide skilled (SNF), intermediate (ICF), and custodial (domiciliary or assisted) care.

If you live in congregate housing for seniors, a retirement community, or a rest home for seniors, the policy should cover care you receive in these facilities as home care. These housing arrangements are considered independent living and are not considered a nursing home. Call your area agency on aging or your state office on aging for a definition of and a list of facilities that fall into one of these categories: nursing home, assisted living, and congregate living. Compare the definitions of these living arrangements with the definition specified in the policy.

Home care also includes adult day health care, which is a special program to care for adults during the day. Adult day service centers providing medical and rehabilitation services are usually covered by home care provisions in long-term care policies. However, you may need only personal services that are provided by social or recreational adult care centers. A policy should not restrict benefits to only adult health care centers.

If you have a primary caregiver, a policy with good home care benefits will help pay for outside help, which will delay the need for a nursing home. Refer to Chapter 3 for a discussion on coverage of home care services. If you do not have a primary caregiver, you may need assisted living or nursing home care even if you would prefer to remain at home. Assisted living facilities are the fastest-growing component of long-term care.

Preexisting Condition

Many of the major companies now immediately cover preexisting conditions as long as they are disclosed on the application. Some policies, however, contain a clause that excludes long-term care services resulting from a preexisting condition until after a waiting period. A preexisting condition is a health problem for which you have received treatment or a condition that manifested itself before buying the policy. The purpose of this clause in a policy is to discourage people from buying a policy because they know they need long-term care.

The waiting period ranges from 3 months to 2 years, with most policies requiring 6 months. The length of the waiting period and definition of a preexisting condition vary among policies. If you think you have a preexisting condition, read the policy very carefully.

Some companies will sell a policy to a person with a preexisting condition that exempts paying for long-term care due to the specific condition. The policy will pay for long-term care *not* due to the specific condition. These limitations to the policy are usually offered to people over 79 years old.

Renewable

Most policies are guaranteed renewable, which means that the company cannot cancel the policy as long as you pay the premiums on time. A few policies are conditionally guaranteed, which means that the company reserves the right to cancel policies for a group of policyholders. So although the company could not cancel just your policy, it could cancel a group in which you are a member.

Waiver of Premiums

After you have received long-term care services for a designated period of time, most policies waive payment of the premiums while you receive benefits. Some policies count the deductible period in the waiver time period; other policies start counting after the deductible period. The designated time period before the waiver is triggered also varies.

Restoration of Benefits

A few companies state that if you do not use any long-term care benefits for 6 full months, the full benefit period is restored. For example, a person with a 3-year benefit period who spends a year in a nursing home will have the full 3 years of benefits restored if the person does not use any long-term care services for 6 months. However, the chance of this happening to an older person is highly unlikely, so it's best not to use this benefit as a basis for selecting a policy.

Consumer Options in Policies

There are several options offered in policies. The preceding sections on how much insurance to buy cautioned about buying too much insurance. The same caution applies to consumer options. Each option selected will increase the premium. You should select options carefully.

Home Care Coverage. Long-term care insurance can pay for needed services in a nursing home, in an assisted living facility, or at home. Integrated policies include home care and assisted living within the overall benefits package, while so-called classic policies offer home care as a rider to a nursing home policy. Before you decide which type of policy you want, think about whether you want home care coverage.

Very few people want to enter a nursing home, preferring to receive care at home. Having a policy that pays for care at home would certainly help. However, is it realistic for you to effectively utilize home care instead of going into a nursing home?

If you have a primary caregiver, usually a spouse, you could effectively use home care services a couple of hours a day, or maybe a couple of days per week. Or you could take advantage of an adult day service center. Your family caregiver could provide the assistance or supervision for the rest of the time. Home care coverage would probably be worthwhile.

If, however, you do not have a caregiver, you may need home care for 8 to 12 hours a day. This would be more expensive than a nursing home. Many policies pay 50 to 80 percent of the nursing home benefit amount for at-home care. The care would be more expensive and the benefit less than if you went into a nursing home. Even with this much home care, you may still encounter problems. Without a caregiver, you will probably not be able to effectively utilize home care services; so buying a policy with home care benefits may not be worthwhile.

The policy should provide benefits if you need long-term care due to physical impairment (one or two ADLs) or cognitive impairment. As Medicare pays for skilled care at home and hospice care, home care coverage should primarily cover personal services from home care aides and personal assistants. Adult day health care should also be covered. Most policies also offer up to 14 days of respite care, which is temporary overnight care that gives a break to the caregiver.

A home care visit is usually 3 to 4 hours. Some policies specify a maximum of 6 hours for a home care visit. In most areas, home care visits or a day at an adult day health center costs about half of the cost of a day in a nursing home. Therefore, many policies provide a home care benefit amount at 50 percent of the nursing home care benefit amount. If you may need more home care than 3 or 4 hours, you might look for a policy that covers home care at 80 to 100 percent of the nursing home benefit. Policies that offer home care as a rider allow you to select the benefit amount you want for home care.

In the case of an integrated policy with which you can draw benefits against a total pool of funds, you should look carefully at whether a home care visit is considered a full day of benefits or whether the actual cost is simply deducted from the pool of benefit money available for long-term care. For example, a 2-year policy at $100 per day could give you 4 years of home care services at $50 per home care visit.

Inflation Adjustment. The advantage of inflation adjustment was discussed in the previous subsection on the benefit amount. That subsection may be worth reading again. For most people an inflation adjustment is a must. Selecting the one for you depends on your circumstances. If you are in your mid-seventies and expect to need long-term care within 5 years, you may want to consider not buying an inflation adjustment. The cost is high, and you will not realize much increase.

If you expect to need long-term care within 10 years, you should consider the option to buy an additional benefit amount. You will save some on premiums while your benefit amount keeps up with inflation.

If you expect to need long-term care within 15 years, you could save a little on the premiums by selecting a simple rate of inflation adjustment. Remember, in 15 years a compound rate of inflation adjustment on a $100-per-day benefit amount pays $33 per day more than a simple rate. You should compare the premium difference to decide if the compound rate is worth the extra cost.

If you expect to need long-term care within 20 years, the compound rate is better. If you expect to need long-term care beyond 20 years, you should also consider a policy that continues the adjustment for the lifetime of the policyholder.

Nonforfeiture Benefit. The converse of the 24 percent probability that you will spend more than a year in a nursing home is a 76 percent probability that you will not. This may sound obvious, but when turned around you realize that you have a greater chance of receiving few or no benefits from your long-term care insurance. You might never need long-term care. Or you might cancel your policy if premiums increase too much, or if your situation changes and you no longer need insurance. Stopping a policy before it pays any benefits is called letting the policy lapse. Pooling insurance risks assumes a certain lapse rate, which lowers the cost of insurance for everyone.

A few companies offer a nonforfeiture benefit in case you lapse the policy. Like any benefit, you pay for it with higher premiums. If you want protection in case you need long-term care, then you are better off buying a lower-priced policy that does not have a nonforfeiture benefit. However, if you harbor some doubt about the eventual need for long-term care, you may want to consider buying this benefit. Nonforfeiture benefits come in several forms.

A return-of-the-premium benefit refunds only a portion of the premiums paid if you die or decide to lapse the policy. The portion is determined by the number of years you paid the premiums. This is the most expensive nonforfeiture benefit. You also pay more for the policy. Therefore, carefully review the added cost of this benefit with the potential amount of premium that will be returned. You may be better off investing the difference instead of buying the policy that returns just some of the money you paid in premiums.

Some policies provide a reduced level of coverage if you cancel your policy because of increased premiums. The benefit period or benefit amount is reduced depending on how long you had the policy. This at least provides some coverage for the money you paid. It is preferable to have a reduced-period benefit for the full benefit amount. This option is less expensive than the return of premium. However, it may not be necessary if you buy a policy that is affordable.

Consumer Tips

Individuals selling long-term care insurance are obviously interested in selling you their policy or, if they are an independent agent or financial planner, a policy from a company with which they are affiliated and from which they receive a commission. That is not to say the policy they recommend is bad; many are good policies. However, you should be aware that the agent is looking for a sale and may not tell you that you might not need insurance or that another plan may be better for you.

Do not rely on the advertising or marketing materials, which are very general. Often marketing materials refer to the policy for explanation of coverage. Ask the agent to see the outline of coverage or a sample policy.

Carefully review each statement on the document with the agent until you are sure you understand the policy. If the agent cannot answer your questions or you still have some concerns, do not sign until you talk to someone else who can answer your questions.

Regardless of what any agent might tell you, if you decide you want long-term care insurance, you only need one policy. Advertising and marketing materials are designed to encourage you to buy long-term care insurance. Do not allow yourself to be pressured. Think through each proposition carefully and do not respond to half-truths or hurry-up tactics. The following are some examples:

While it is true that premiums are lower at a younger age, it also means you are paying for a longer period of time. For one $80-per-day, 3-year policy, the premium at age 55 is $700 per year, and at age 75, the premium is $3,500 per year. If two individuals, one age 55 and the other age 75, pay their premiums until age 85, the one who bought at age 75 will pay $35,000 while the one who started at age 55 will pay $21,000, almost half as much.

Advantages to buying at a younger age are (1) lower annual and possibly total premiums; and (2) protection for an early, unexpected need for long-term care. However, there are disadvantages. The longer you pay, the greater the likelihood of increases in premiums and changes in public policy. Paying premiums for insurance means you cannot use the money for other purposes or leave it for an inheritance. You should also know that rates are lower at a younger age because you have a higher probability of dying before the policy pays off.

Nursing home costs vary. If the agent tells you that the payment of $80 a day pays for most of the daily cost in a nursing home, investigate the cost of nursing homes in your community. Determine if that policy's per diem payment is realistic.

A stay in a nursing home costs more than the facility's quoted daily rate. In addition, you will need to pay for items such as medications, insurance premiums for Medicare Part B and possibly a medigap policy, doctors' fees if you do not have medical insurance, personal services such as hair permanents or laundry, and perhaps even special medical supplies and equipment.

Also remember that nursing home costs continue to increase. In the example above, the individual buying at age 55 and entering a nursing home at age 85 has 30 years of inflation. Just think how prices in general have risen in the past 30 years. Prices in the next 30 years most likely will increase at least as much.

If you want to hedge against inflation, buy a policy that adjusts the per diem amount with inflation. You will pay more for this type of coverage, but it is generally worth it. First, talk to your children and discuss your financial concerns and the options presented in this guide. Your children are not financially responsible to pay for your long-term care. A policy will not prevent you from needing long-term care, nor the guilt family will feel about having a loved one go into a nursing home even if a policy is paying for it, nor the time and emotional drain on your children in finding and monitoring long-term care services. Consider what would happen if you do not buy the insurance and instead invest the amount of the premium or spend it on yourself or your family.

Insurance is for people who have an estate to protect and who have the income now and in the future to pay the premiums. It is not for people who must use their savings to pay the premium, nor is it for people with only modest savings. No magic, universally applicable dollar amount exists to define the minimum-size estate you should have before considering insurance. In the simple scenario described in this chapter's section on financial resources, insurance began to make economic sense for a couple with one spouse in a nursing home and with an annual income of $15,000 and $50,000 in assets, excluding their residence and car, and above the maximum Medicaid asset limit of roughly $84,000. According to this scenario, when income and assets are below these amounts, insurance benefits overlap with Medicaid payments. This would relieve Medicaid of cost, not you. Depending on your financial situation, insurance does not prevent your requiring Medicaid assistance; it only delays it. Your financial circumstances and plans are unique to you, and so you need to calculate at what point insurance makes most economic sense for you.

A reputable insurance company will not pressure you to make a decision. Ask the agent to leave material with you, and make clear that you need time to review and analyze it before you make any decisions. Even after you have considered the proposal and applied for the insurance, you have 30 days from the delivery date of the contract to examine it and return it for a full refund. This is called the 30-day free-look period. In any case, do not allow the agent to rush you. This is an important decision that you should take your time considering. If the agent insists on a quick decision, your answer should be "No thanks." There are plenty of reputable people who can obtain this kind of policy for you.

Sources that can be of assistance in understanding policy issues include insurance agents and brokers, elder-law attorneys, and the senior health insurance counseling programs in your state.

For Your Information

Health Insurance Association of America (HIAA)
1201 F Street, NW, Suite 500
Washington, DC 20004-1109
Phone: 800-879-4422
Web site: www.hiaa.org

HIAA is a trade association representing health insurance companies. HIAA produces a free brochure entitled "Guide to Long-Term Care Insurance" that lists companies selling long-term care insurance.

Long-Term Care Insurance Educational Foundation
PO Box 370
Centerville, VA 20122
Phone: 703-968-8868
Web site: www.ltcedfoundation.org

The Long-Term Care Insurance Educational Foundation is a nonprofit organization. Its purpose is to plan and execute a national conference focused on public policy issues affecting the development of the private long-term care insurance market.

National Association of Insurance Commissioners (NAIC)
2301 McGee Street, Suite 800
Kansas City, MO 64108
Phone: 816-842-3600
Web site: www.naic.org

NAIC represents state insurance regulators. Write for a free copy of the pamphlet "Shopper's Guide to Long-Term Care Insurance."

For a list of companies authorized to sell long-term care insurance policies in the state in which you reside, contact your state insurance department.

United Seniors Health Council (USHC)
409 Third Street, SW
Washington, DC 20024-3212
Phone: 800-637-2604
Web site: www.unitedseniorshealth.org

USHC has available the 145-page book *Long-Term Care Insurance. A Professional's Guide to Selecting Policies*. To order, send a check for $41 (includes shipping and handling) to USHC or order by phone with an American Express, VISA, or MasterCard.

Weiss Ratings, Inc.
4176 Burns Road
Palm Beach Gardens, FL 33410
Phone: 800-289-9222
Web site: www.weissratings.com

Weiss provides safety ratings evaluating the financial stability of insurance companies and banks and brokers as well as the risk-adjusted performance of mutual funds and common stocks. Call today or visit Weiss's Web site for more information.

Conclusion

For most of their lives, people avoid serious discussion and planning about how they will pay for long-term care. The reasons for this avoidance are many. Some people are unaware of their future need for long-term care services; others dislike financial planning for the future; and many are so overwhelmed by the problem, they are reluctant to tackle it. As a result, people find themselves scrambling around at the last minute trying to understand and solve the problem or, even worse, become caught in a quagmire of impoverishment.

This guide does not claim to contain all the solutions to all the problems. It, however, has highlighted the primary long-term care issues facing older people, and it has described many long-term care services and where you can find assistance. The pros and cons of various common as well as innovative options for long-term care have also been presented.

Financing long-term care and managing long-term care assistance are issues for society as well as for individuals. No single, magic formula exists for meeting the long-term care needs of the country or of a particular older person. Each person's financial, physical, and social situation is unique and changes over time. Therefore, each older person and his or her family should create a customized long-term care plan and should review it periodically as circumstances warrant.

Like the situation of a particular individual, public financial priorities and assistance programs shift. The benefits and terms of today's government-supported programs such as Medicaid or those provided under the Older Americans Act may well be different tomorrow.

Similarly, private responses to long-term care needs change. For example, long-term care insurance and reverse mortgage plans have evolved, and new wrinkles in these products will continue to be introduced.

What does all this mean for you as an individual? First, whatever your age, you should not delay at least in considering the prospect of long-term care and preferably in developing a plan. Second, you should prepare for change and have flexibility to modify your plan in response to any changes in your own situation as well as in public programs available to assist with long-term care.

In conclusion, as you shape your long-term care plan, you should keep in mind the following general guidelines.

1. Use this and other publications to educate yourself about government programs and private initiatives for financing long-term care. There is no substitute for being an informed consumer. Reading this guide is a good start in knowing your options.
2. Think creatively about how you can use available resources, including your family, your home, and community services, to remain independent in your own home for as long as possible. This guide will stimulate you to think about other possibilities.
3. Become knowledgeable about Medicaid, the federal-state–sponsored financial assistance to pay for health, medical, and long-term care needs of people who cannot afford to pay for them. Although Medicaid is not a good solution, for many older persons it is the only option available. You worked hard all your life and have helped finance this public program through tax contributions. It is only fair that if you need assistance and you qualify, you should use it.
4. Concerning long-term care insurance, let the buyer beware. First you have to decide whether you need long-term care insurance. If you do, and many people do not, then read very carefully each policy you are considering, making sure you understand what it does *not* cover before you buy. Long-term care policies contain differing restrictions and limitations that may affect your ability to claim benefits later. Take care to buy a policy that is the most likely to meet your own future needs.

5. Discuss the material in this guide with family and loved ones. You may be surprised at their feelings and recommendations.

6. Let your elected officials know that you are concerned about government responses to the nation's long-term care needs and that developing a comprehensive care solution should be a priority.

A

Long-Term Care Insurance Worksheet

This worksheet will help you compare long-term care insurance policies. Refer to "Which Policy Is Right for Me?" in Chapter 7 for a discussion of questions you should ask.

	POLICY A	POLICY B	POLICY C
1. Company name and policy number	_____	_____	_____
2. Deductible/elimination period (number of days)	_____	_____	_____
3. Benefit daily amount paid			
Nursing home care	_____	_____	_____
Home care	_____	_____	_____
Assisted living	_____	_____	_____
Adult day care	_____	_____	_____
Respite care	_____	_____	_____
4. Inflation adjustment			
Inflation rate (%)	_____	_____	_____
Simple or compounded	_____	_____	_____
Option to buy additional benefit amount	_____	_____	_____
How often applied? (years)	_____	_____	_____
For how long?	_____	_____	_____
If not included in premium, price for option	_____	_____	_____
5. Maximum amount of benefits (indicate in days or dollar amount)	_____	_____	_____
6. Requirements for coverage			
Prior hospitalization (yes/no)	_____	_____	_____
Medically necessary/illness, injury (yes/no)	_____	_____	_____
Activities of daily living (ADLs) (how many?)	_____	_____	_____
Which ADLs? How defined?	_____	_____	_____
Cognitive impairment (yes/no)	_____	_____	_____
Linked to ADLs or medical necessity? (yes/no)	_____	_____	_____
7. Coverage for Alzheimer's disease, a type of cognitive impairment? (yes/no)	_____	_____	_____
Is coverage linked to ADLs or medical necessity (yes/no)	_____	_____	_____

	POLICY A	POLICY B	POLICY C
8. Preexisting condition			
Immediately covered if disclosed on application? (yes/no)	_____	_____	_____
If not, definition	_____	_____	_____
Waiting period	_____	_____	_____
9. Level of care (yes/no)			
Skilled	_____	_____	_____
Intermediate	_____	_____	_____
Custodial	_____	_____	_____
Home care aides	_____	_____	_____
Assisted living	_____	_____	_____
Adult day care	_____	_____	_____
Respite care	_____	_____	_____
10. What is not covered?	_____	_____	_____
11. Guarantee renewable (yes/no)	_____	_____	_____
(Unconditional guarantee is preferable)	_____	_____	_____
12. Premiums level (yes/no)	_____	_____	_____
13. Premiums waived			
For nursing home care? (yes/no)	_____	_____	_____
For home health care?	_____	_____	_____
Time period for waiver	_____	_____	_____
14. Company rating			
A.M. Best	_____	_____	_____
Standard & Poor's	_____	_____	_____
Duff & Phelps	_____	_____	_____
Moody's	_____	_____	_____
Weiss	_____	_____	_____
15. Benefit amount	_____	_____	_____
Benefit period	_____	_____	_____
16. Premium—monthly	_____	_____	_____
Premium—annually	_____	_____	_____

B

State Health Insurance Assistance Programs

This list was provided by the U.S. Department of Health and Human Services' Centers for Medicare and Medicaid Services (CMS).

The State Health Insurance Assistance Program, or SHIP, is a national program that offers one-on-one counseling and assistance to people with Medicare and their families. Through grants from CMS directed to states, SHIPs provide free counseling and assistance via telephone and face–to-face interactive sessions, public education presentations and programs, and media activities. To find the location nearest you, phone the number listed for your state, territory, or district, or call 1-800-633-4227, or search on the Internet at www.medicare.gov.

State or Area	Phone	State or Area	Phone
Alabama	800-243-5463	Montana	800-332-2272
Alaska	800-478-6065	Nebraska	800-234-7119
American Samoa	888-875-9229	Nevada	800-307-4444
Arizona	800-432-4040	New Hampshire	800-852-3388
Arkansas	800-224-6330	New Jersey	800-792-8820
California	800-434-0222	New Mexico	800-432-2080
Colorado	888-696-7213	New York	800-333-4114
Connecticut	800-994-9422	North Carolina	800-443-9354
Delaware	800-336-9500	North Dakota	800-247-0560
District of Columbia	202-739-0668	Northern Mariana Islands	888-875-9229
Florida	800-963-5337	Ohio	800-686-1578
Georgia	800-669-8387	Oklahoma	800-763-2828
Guam	888-875-9229	Oregon	800-722-4134
Hawaii	888-875-9229	Pennsylvania	800-783-7067
Idaho	800-247-4422	Puerto Rico	877-725-4300
Illinois	800-548-9034	Rhode Island	401-222-2880
Indiana	800-452-4800	South Carolina	800-868-9095
Iowa	800-351-4664	South Dakota	800-822-8804
Kansas	800-860-5260	Tennessee	877-801-0044
Kentucky	877-293-7447	Texas	800-252-9240
Louisiana	800-259-5301	Utah	800-439-3805
Maine	800-750-5323	Vermont	800-642-5119
Maryland	800-243-3425	Virgin Islands	340-772-7368
Massachusetts	800-882-2003	Washington	800-397-4422
Michigan	800-803-7174	West Virginia	800-642-9004
Minnesota	800-333-2433	Wisconsin	800-242-1060
Mississippi	800-948-3090	Wyoming	800-856-4398
Missouri	800-390-3330		

C

State Insurance Departments

This list was provided by the National Association of Insurance Commissioners.

Alabama
**Alabama Department of
    Insurance**
201 Monroe Street, Suite 1700
Montgomery, AL 36104
334-269-3550
Fax: 334-241-4192

Alaska
Alaska Division of Insurance
3601 C Street, Suite 1324
Anchorage, AK 99503-5948
907-269-7900
Fax: 907-269-7912

American Samoa
Office of the Governor
American Samoa Government
Pago Pago, American Samoa
    96799
011-684-633-4116
Fax: 011-684-633-2269

Arizona
Arizona Department of Insurance
2910 North 44th Street, Suite 210
Phoenix, AZ 85018-7256
602-912-8400
Fax: 602-912-8452

Arkansas
**Arkansas Department of
    Insurance**
1200 West 3rd Street
Little Rock, AR 72201-1904
501-371-2600
Fax: 501-371-2629

California
**California Department of
    Insurance**
300 Capitol Mall, Suite 1500
Sacramento, CA 95814
916-492-3500
Fax: 916-445-5280

Colorado
Colorado Division of Insurance
1560 Broadway, Suite 850
Denver, CO 80202
303-894-7499
Fax: 303-894-7455

Connecticut
**Connecticut Department of
    Insurance**
PO Box 816
Hartford, CT 06142-0816
860-297-3800
Fax: 860-566-7410

Delaware
**Delaware Department of
    Insurance**
Rodney Building
841 Silver Lake Boulevard
Dover, DE 19904
302-739-4251
Fax: 302-739-5280

District of Columbia
**Department of Insurance &
    Securities Regulation**
Government of the District of
    Columbia
810 First Street, NE,
    Suite 701
Washington, DC 20002
202-727-8000 Ext. 3018
Fax: 202-535-1196

Florida
Florida Department of Insurance
State Capitol
Plaza Level Eleven
Tallahassee, FL 32399-0300
850-413-2804
Fax: 850-413-2950

Georgia
Georgia Department of Insurance
2 Martin Luther King, Jr. Drive
Floyd Memorial Building
704 West Tower
Atlanta, GA 30334
404-656-2056
Fax: 404-657-7493

Guam
**Department of Revenue &
    Taxation**
Insurance Branch
Government of Guam
Building 13-3, 1st Floor
Mariner Avenue
Tiyan, Barrigada, GU 96913
671-475-1843
Fax: 671-472-2643

Hawaii
Hawaii Insurance Division
Department of Commerce &
    Consumer Affairs
250 South King Street, 5th Floor
Honolulu, HI 96813
808-586 2790
Fax: 808-586-2806

Idaho
Idaho Department of Insurance
700 West State Street, 3rd Floor
Boise, ID 83720-0043
208-334-4250
Fax: 208-334-4398

Illinois
Illinois Department of Insurance
320 West Washington Street,
    4th Floor
Springfield, IL 62767-0001
217-782-4515
Fax: 217-524-6500

Indiana
Indiana Department of Insurance
311 West Washington Street,
    Suite 300
Indianapolis, IN 46204-2787
317-232-2385
Fax: 317-232-5251

Iowa
Division of Insurance
State of Iowa
330 East Maple Street
Des Moines, IA 50319
515-281-5705
Fax: 515-281-3059

Kansas
Kansas Department of Insurance
420 SW 9th Street
Topeka, KS 66612-1678
785-296-7801
Fax: 785-296-2283

Kentucky
**Kentucky Department of
    Insurance**
PO Box 517
215 West Main Street
Frankfort, KY 40602-0517
502-564-6027
Fax: 502-564-1453

Louisiana
**Louisiana Department of
    Insurance**
950 North 5th Street
Baton Rouge, LA 70802
225-342-5423
Fax: 225-342-8622

Maine
Maine Bureau of Insurance
Department of Professional &
    Financial Regulation
State Office Building, Station 34
Augusta, ME 04333-0034
207-624-8475
Fax: 207-624-8599

Maryland
**Maryland Insurance
    Administration**
525 St. Paul Place
Baltimore, MD 21202-2272
410-468-2090
Fax: 410-468-2020

Massachusetts
Division of Insurance
Commonwealth of Massachusetts
One South Station, 4th Floor
Boston, MA 02110
617-521-7301
Fax: 617-521-7758

Michigan
**Office of Financial and Insurance
    Services**
State of Michigan
611 West Ottawa Street,
    2nd Floor North
Lansing, MI 48933-1020
517-335-3167
Fax: 517-373-4870

Minnesota
**Minnesota Department of
    Commerce**
85 7th Place East, Suite 500
St. Paul, MN 55101-2198
651-296-6025
Fax: 651-282-2568

Mississippi
Mississippi Insurance Department
501 North West Street
Woolfolk State Office Building,
    10th Floor
Jackson, MS 39201
601-359-3569
Fax: 601-359-2474

Missouri
Missouri Department of Insurance
301 West High Street, Suite 530
Jefferson City, MO 65101
573-751-4126
Fax: 573-751-1165

Montana
**Montana Department of
Insurance**
840 Helena Avenue
Helena, MT 59601
406-444-2040
Fax: 406-444-3497

Nebraska
**Nebraska Department of
Insurance**
Terminal Building, Suite 400
941 'O' Street
Lincoln, NE 68508
402-471-2201
Fax: 402-471-4610

Nevada
Nevada Division of Insurance
788 Fairview Drive, Suite 300
Carson City, NV 89701-5753
775-687-4270
Fax: 775-687-3937

New Hampshire
Department of Insurance
State of New Hampshire
56 Old Suncook Road
Concord, NH 03301
603-271-2261
Fax: 603-271-1406

New Jersey
**New Jersey Department of
Insurance**
20 West State Street CN325
Trenton, NJ 08625
609-292-5360
Fax: 609 984-5273

New Mexico
**New Mexico Department of
Insurance**
PO Drawer 1269
Santa Fe, NM 87504-1269
505-827-4601
Fax: 505-476-0326

New York
**New York Department of
Insurance**
25 Beaver Street
New York, NY 10004-2319
212-480-2292
Fax: 212-480-2310

North Carolina
**North Carolina Department of
Insurance**
PO Box 26387
Raleigh, NC 27611
919-733-3058
Fax: 919-733-6495

North Dakota
**North Dakota Department of
Insurance**
600 East Boulevard
Bismarck, ND 58505-0320
701-328-2440
Fax: 701-328-4880

Ohio
Ohio Department of Insurance
2100 Stella Court
Columbus, OH 43215-1067
614-644-2658
Fax: 614-644-3743

Oklahoma
**Oklahoma Department of
    Insurance**
2401 NW 23rd Street, Suite 28
Oklahoma City, OK 73107
405-521-2828
Fax: 405-521-6635

Oregon
Oregon Insurance Division
350 Winter Street NE, Room 440
Salem, OR 97310-3883
503-947-7980
Fax: 503-378-4351

Pennsylvania
**Pennsylvania Insurance
    Department**
1326 Strawberry Square, 13th
    Floor
Harrisburg, PA 17120
717-783-0442
Fax: 717-772-1969

Puerto Rico
**Puerto Rico Department of
    Insurance**
Cobian's Plaza Building
1607 Ponce de Leon Avenue
Santurce, PR 00909
787-722-8686
Fax: 787-722-4400

Rhode Island
Rhode Island Insurance Division
Department of Business
    Regulation
233 Richmond Street,
    Suite 233
Providence, RI 02903-4233
401-222-2223
Fax: 401-222-5475

South Carolina
**South Carolina Department of
    Insurance**
300 Arbor Lake Drive,
    Suite 1200
Columbia, SC 29223
803-737-6160
Fax: 803-737-6229

South Dakota
**South Dakota Division of
    Insurance**
Department of Commerce &
    Regulation
118 West Capitol Avenue
Pierre, SD 57501-2000
605-773-3563
Fax: 605-773-5369

Tennessee
**Tennessee Department of
    Commerce & Insurance**
Davy Crockett Tower, Fifth Floor
500 James Robertson Parkway
Nashville, TN 37243-0565
615-741-2241
Fax: 615-532-6934

Texas
Texas Department of Insurance
333 Guadalupe Street
Austin, TX 78701
Consumer helpline: 800-252-3439
512-463-6464
Fax: 512-475-2005

Utah
Utah Department of Insurance
3110 State Office Building
Salt Lake City, UT 84114-1201
801-538-3800
Fax: 801-538-3829

Vermont
Vermont Division of Insurance
Department of Banking, Insurance
   & Securities
89 Main Street, Drawer 20
Montpelier, VT 05620-3101
802-828-3301
Fax: 802-828-3306

Virgin Islands
**Division of Banking and
   Insurance**
1131 King Street, Suite 101
St. Croix, VI 00820
340-773-6449
Fax: 340-773-4052

Virginia
State Corporation Commission
Bureau of Insurance
Commonwealth of Virginia
PO Box 1157
Richmond, VA 23218
804-371-9694
Fax: 804-371-9873

Washington
**Washington Office of the
   Insurance Commissioner**
14th Avenue and Water Street
PO Box 40255
Olympia, WA 98504-0255
360-664-8137
Fax: 360-586-3535

West Virginia
**West Virginia Department of
   Insurance**
PO Box 50540
Charleston, WV 25305-0540
304-558-3354
Fax: 304-558-0412

Wisconsin
**Office of the Commissioner of
   Insurance**
State of Wisconsin
121 East Wilson
Madison, WI 53702
608-267-1233
Fax: 608-261-8579

Wyoming
**Wyoming Department of
   Insurance**
Herschler Building
122 West 25th Street, 3rd East
Cheyenne, WY 82002-0440
307-777-7401
Fax: 307-777-5895

D

Companies Selling Long-Term Care Insurance

This list of their members was provided by the Health Insurance Association of America (HIAA). HIAA is the trade association representing the private health care system. HIAA does not endorse particular products; it provides this directory as an informational service for consumers. Companies listed in this guide have all identified themselves as actively marketing long-term care insurance. However, companies may not be licensed in all jurisdictions, so consumers should contact individual companies for more information.

Allianz Life Insurance Company of North America
1750 Hennepin Avenue
Minneapolis, MN 55447
800-328-5601
www.allianzlife.com

American Family Life Assurance Company of Columbus (AFLAC)
1932 Wynnton Road
Columbus, GA 31999
800-992-3588
www.aflac.com

American Family Mutual Insurance Company
6000 American Parkway
Madison, WI 53783
800-333-6886
www.amfam.com

American Fidelity Assurance Company
2000 North Classen Boulevard
PO Box 268842
Oklahoma City, OK 73106
888-412-2121
www.af-group.com/ltc

American Heritage Life Insurance Company
1776 American Heritage Life Drive
Jacksonville, FL 32224
800-780-3724
www.AHL1776.com

American Republic Insurance Company
601 6th Avenue
PO Box 9393
Des Moines, IA 50306-9514
888-922-2975
www.americanrepublic.com

Bankers Life and Casualty Company
(A Conseco Company)
222 Merchandise Mart Plaza
Chicago, IL 60654-2001
888-282-8252
www.bankerslife.com

Bankers United Life Assurance Company
(Member of AEGON Insurance Group)
2705 Brown Trail
Bedford, TX 76021
800-322-1434
www.aegonins.com

Blue Cross Life & Health
2100 Corporate Center Drive
Newbury Park, CA 91320
805-480-7289
www.bluecrossca.com

Central States Health and Life Company of Omaha
96th and Western
PO Box 34350
Omaha, NE 68134-0350
800-732-4595 Ext. 6000
www.cso.com

CNA
PO Box 305090
Nashville, TN 37230
800-262-2952
www.cnaltc.com

Combined Insurance Company of America
5050 North Broadway
Chicago, IL 60640
800-999-2170
www.combinedinsurance.com

Combined Life Insurance Company of New York
11 British American Boulevard
Latham, NY 12110
800-951-6206
www.combinedinsurance.com

Conseco Health Insurance Company, and Conseco Senior Health Insurance Company
11825 North Pennsylvania Street
Carmel, IN 46082-1911
800-772-6881
www.conseco.com

Continental General Insurance Company
8901 Indian Hills Drive
PO Box 247007
Omaha, NE 68124-7007
800-545-8905
agency@continentalgeneral.com

Country Life Insurance Company
1711 G.E. Road
Bloomington, IL 61704
800-676-0319
www.countrycompanies.com

General Electric Capital Assurance Company
GE Capital Life Assurance Company of New York
LTC Division
1650 Los Gamos Drive
San Rafael, CA 94903
800-456-7766
www.gefn.com/longtermcare

Guarantee Trust Life Insurance Company
1275 Milwaukee Avenue
Glenview, IL 60025
800-338-7452
www.gtlic.com

John Hancock Financial Services
200 Clarendon Street
Boston, MA 02117
800-695-7389
www.jhancock.com

Life Investors Insurance Company of America
(Member of AEGON Insurance Group)
2705 Brown Trail
Bedford, TX 76021
800-325-5823
www.aegonins.com

MedAmerica Insurance Company
165 Court Street
Rochester, NY 14647
800-544-0327
www.yourlongtermcare.com

Metropolitan Life Insurance Company (MetLife)
Long-Term Care Group
PO Box 937
Westport, CT 06881-0937
800-308-0179
www.metlife.com

Monumental Life Insurance Company
(Member of AEGON Insurance Group)
2705 Brown Trail
Bedford, TX 76021
800-845-3695
www.aegonins.com

Mutual of Omaha
Mutual of Omaha Plaza
Omaha, NE 68175
800-775-6000
www.mutualofomaha.com

New York Life
New York Life Administration Corporation
98 San Jacinto Boulevard, Suite 800
Austin, TX 78701
800-224-4582
www.newyorklifeltc.com

Northwestern Long Term Care Insurance Company (A subsidiary of Northwestern Mutual)
720 East Wisconsin Avenue
Milwaukee, WI 53202
877-582-6582 (toll-free)
www.northwesternmutual.com

Penn Treaty Network America Insurance Company
3440 Lehigh Street
Allentown, PA 18103
800-222-3469
www.penntreaty.com

Peoples Benefit Life Insurance Company
(Member of AEGON Insurance Group)
2705 Brown Trail
Bedford, TX 76021
800-698-7851
www.aegonins.com

PFL Life Insurance Company
(Member of AEGON Insurance Group)
2705 Brown Trail
Bedford, TX 76021
800-338-0257
www.aegonins.com

Physicians Mutual Insurance Company
2600 Dodge Street
Omaha, NE 68131
800-645-4300
www.pmic.com

Pioneer Life Insurance Company
(A Conseco Company)
11825 North Pennsylvania Street
PO Box 1911
Carmel, IN 46032
800-759-7007
www.conseco.com

Pyramid Life Insurance Company
6201 Johnson Drive
Mission, KS 66202-3396
800-777-1126
www.pyramidlife.com

Standard Life and Accident Insurance Company
Marina Plaza
2450 South Shore Boulevard, Suite 501
League City, TX 77573-2417
888-290-1085
www.anico.com

State Farm Insurance Company
One State Farm Plaza
Bloomington, IL 61710
Call local agent for information
www.statefarm.com

Teachers Protective Mutual Life Insurance Company
116-118 North Prince Street
Lancaster, PA 17603
800-555-3122
www.tpmins.com

TIAA-CREF
730 Third Avenue
New York, NY 10017
800-223-1200
www.tiaa-cref.org

Transamerica Occidental Life Insurance Company
(Member of AEGON Insurance Group)
2705 Brown Trail
Bedford, TX 76021
800-227-3740
www.transamerica.com

Trigon Blue Cross Blue Shield
602 South Jefferson Street
Roanoke, VA 24011
888-208-1870
www.trigon.com

Trustmark Insurance Company
400 Field Drive
Lakeforest, IL 60045
800-947-8888
www.trustmarkins.com

Index

The National Council on the Aging (NCOA)

Always go to the leading expert...and that's why you should join NCOA.

NCOA is...

- A national advocate for aging-related issues
- A leader in the development of innovative programs
- A reservoir of expertise on important aging issues
- A community of professionals
- A resource center

And, NCOA benefits are targeted to helping individuals and organizations who work with older adults.

Here are 5 Reasons Why NCOA Membership is a real BENEFIT!

1. **Advocacy**
   NCOA brings you up-to-the-minute information about legislation and information issues through regular **Public Policy Updates** and **Action Alerts**; expert representation before lawmakers on senior and community service issues; access to our Web-based software that enables you to easily contact your members of Congress and the local press as well as track critical legislation. Finally, join your colleagues in our online public policy and advocacy discussion bulletin boards.

2. Publications

NCOA provides you with resources that include our quarterly publication *Innovations*; *NCOA Week*, a weekly e-mail newsletter that includes new resources and developments that affect the field of aging; online bulletin boards; a Senior Center Accreditation Program; a monthly Workforce Report e-newsletter, which provides breaking news in workforce development for older workers; and best practices information. Plus much more!

3. Innovative Programs

NCOA programs range from the **Family Friends Program**, which is now part of the fabric of dozens of communities nationwide, to NCOA's newest program, **Benefits***CheckUp*, which provides immediate online access to seniors and caregivers on benefits. NCOA's ongoing commitment to develop and promote innovative programs is unrivaled. Members help us develop and test these programs, and they are among the first to gain access to them.

4. Conferences and Training Opportunities

The joint NCOA/ASA Conference is the major annual opportunity for learning, sharing, and forging new partnerships. Plus, through NCOA Constituent Unit activities, you can focus on your special interests and learn more.

5. Ten Special Interest Groups

If you're interested in health promotion, adult day services, older workers, rural aging, long-term care, financial services, senior centers, senior housing, or interfaith aging issues, NCOA's ten constituent units offer members a unique opportunity. You can focus on these topics, learn about programs that work, and be counted as part of this unique community.

Want more information about NCOA programs and member benefits? To join, visit our Web site at www.ncoa.org or call 202-479-6666.

The National Council on the Aging, Inc.
409 Third Street, SW
Washington, DC 20024

A Message from Charles Mondin, Director of United Seniors Health Council

Thank you for your recent purchase of *Planning for Long-Term Care* prepared by United Seniors Health Council (USHC), a program of The National Council on the Aging. USHC provides you with up-to-date, objective information so that you may make wise decisions about your health care and how to pay for it. We research the material carefully and then have it reviewed by knowledgeable professionals and consumers like you. If you have suggestions as to how we can improve this publication, please let us know. We take readers' comments very seriously.

Let me invite you to subscribe to our quarterly newsletter, *United Seniors Health Report*. Each issue of the *Health Report* contains timely information on topics such as changes in insurance (Medicare, medigap, HMOs, and long-term care insurance); trends to be aware of in living arrangements (such as assisted living or life care communities); changes being discussed in Congress that may affect you; new treatments for health conditions; and helpful suggestions that promote healthy lifestyles.

Subscribing to the newsletter will bring you other advantages as well. Each year you will receive USHC's annual *Medicare Health Plan Choices: Consumer Update* so that you can be sure you have the best health insurance coverage to fit your needs and your pocketbook.

Normally there is a charge for this annual update, but it is free to subscribers of the *Health Report*.

You are also eligible to participate in Medical Bill Minder, a medical bill-claims service. This service will take care of filing claims for you and monitoring the situation to be sure that you are getting all the reimbursements you are entitled to receive. The basic service is $18 a month, invaluable for those who are receiving multiple bills for a variety of medical services and lack the time or the strength to follow up on each one. For more information, or to enroll, call Medical Business Associates toll-free at 888-236 7172—be sure to mention USHC.

I invite you to subscribe to *United Seniors Health Report* by completing the following order form. For just $20 a year, or a little more than 5 cents a day, you can make a wise investment in your good health.

Detach and mail to: USHC, 409 Third Street, SW, Washington, DC 20024

☐ I wish to order a one-year subscription to USHC's quarterly newsletter, *United Seniors Health Report*, for $20.

Name _____

Organization (if applicable) _____

Street/PO Box _____

City _____ State _____ Zip _____

Phone_____ Fax _____

E-mail _____

Method of Payment:

☐ Check (payable to NCOA)   ☐ Purchase Order

☐ Credit Card: ☐ American Express   ☐ MasterCard   ☐ VISA

Account No. _____ Exp. Date _____

Signature _____

Or fax this form to 202-479-6660 or call 800-637-2604 to subscribe.